# Cambridge English

# Objective First

## Workbook
### with answers

Annette Capel   Wendy Sharp                **Fourth Edition**

# CAMBRIDGE
### UNIVERSITY PRESS

University Printing House, Cambridge CB2 8BS, United Kingdom

One Liberty Plaza, 20th Floor, New York, NY 10006, USA

477 Williamstown Road, Port Melbourne, VIC 3207, Australia

314–321, 3rd Floor, Plot 3, Splendor Forum, Jasola District Centre, New Delhi – 110025, India

103 Penang Road, #05-06/07, Visioncrest Commercial, Singapore 238467

Cambridge University Press is part of the University of Cambridge.

It furthers the University's mission by disseminating knowledge in the pursuit of education, learning and research at the highest international levels of excellence.

www.cambridge.org
Information on this title: www.cambridge.org/9781107628458

First published 2000
Second edition 2008
Third edition 2012
Fourth edition 2014

20  19  18

Printed in Great Britain by Ashford Colour Press Ltd.

*A catalogue for this publication is available from the British Library*

| | |
|---|---|
| ISBN 978-1-107-62845-8 | Workbook with answers with Audio CD |
| ISBN 978-1-107-62839-7 | Workbook without answers with Audio CD |
| ISBN 978-1-107-62834-2 | Student's Book without answers with CD-ROM |
| ISBN 978-1-107-62830-4 | Student's Book with answers with CD-ROM |
| ISBN 978-1-107-62835-9 | Teacher's Book with Teacher's Resources CD-ROM |
| ISBN 978-1-107-62854-0 | Class Audio CDs (2) |
| ISBN 978-1-107-62856-4 | Student's Pack (Student's Book without answers with CD-ROM, Workbook without answers with Audio CD) |
| ISBN 978-1-107-62847-2 | Student's Book Pack (Student's Book with answers with CD-ROM and Class Audio CDs (2)) |
| ISBN 978-1-107-29696-1 | Student's Book ebook |
| ISBN 978-1-107-62857-1 | Presentation Plus DVD-ROM |

Additional resources for this publication at www.cambridge.org/elt/objectivefirstnew

Cover concept by Tim Elcock

Produced by Hart McLeod Ltd., Cambridge

# Contents

# Fashion matters

## Vocabulary

### Spellcheck

1 *Clothes Show Live* is a huge fashion exhibition that takes place every December in Birmingham. Read this extract from the catalogue proofs. Check the spelling before it goes to print! An example is given. There are ten more errors to correct.

---

## STANDS IN HALL 6

### Elite Premier Model Agency

*modelling*
For a career in ~~modeling~~. You could become the next supermodel!

### Express

Get some free advice on your hairstile.
Make-up demonstrations too.

### Cool Accessories

The brightest and most outragous designer bags!
Fantastic headgear too, including stylish caps and hats.

### |Gemini|

Gemini makes beautiful jewelery from crystals and gemstones, including braclets, earings and pendants. And it's less expensiv than you might think!

### Simply Leather

An exiting range of leather clothing, from casual jackets to the smartest suites. Watches, belts, bags and sunglasses also available.

###  LoveBomb

Unisex clubwear for the really fashion-conscius, with diferent abstract prints that glow in the dark!

---

2 **Correct the spelling errors in these sentences written by exam candidates.**

a You can immagine how excited I was.
b There is a beautifull view from up there.
c The concert was briliant.
d This was only the beggining.
e According to the writter, it is expensive.
f They did not appologise for this.
g I hope you weren't dissapointed.
h Hapiness is the most important thing.

### Phrasal verbs

3 **Complete the following sentences with phrasal verbs from the box in an appropriate form.**

| | | |
|---|---|---|
| dress up | get away with | keep up with |
| pull on | put together | smarten up | stand out |

a I go to at least ten big fashion shows a year, just to ..................................... the latest designs.
b Joan asked me to paint the flat with her, so I ..................................... an old sweatshirt and my tattiest pair of jeans.
c Henry could ..................................... wearing jeans in his last job, but now he has had to ..................................... himself ..................................... .
d Nigel ..................................... for the party, but when he arrived, he really ..................................... , as everyone else was wearing casual clothes.
e Alice has ..................................... an amazing outfit using recycled clothing and glass beads.

# Reading

**4** Look at the photo of a pair of jeans. How old do you think they are? Read the text quickly to find out.

$25,000 may sound excessive for a tatty pair of jeans, but the ones in this picture are not an ordinary pair of Levi's. They are said to be one of the two oldest pairs left. They are certainly the most expensive!

Discovered last year in an old coal mine in Colorado, they were initially sold for $10,000 and then sold on again at a higher price. Then Seth Weisser paid even more for them. Co-owner of a store appropriately called *What Comes Around Goes Around*, he decided to contact Levi's in San Francisco. 'I sent them pictures of the jeans and they were delighted. They would have paid $40,000, I think!'

Levi's has its own museum and Lynn Downey, the company historian, said:

'I knew this would be a treasure that everyone in the company would want us to have, so Levi's agreed to pay one of the highest sums ever for a pair of old jeans.'

Apart from a hole in the left pocket and frayed edges at the bottom, the jeans are in remarkably good condition for their age. Ms Downey was able to date them by their leather patch, which was added in 1886, and the single back pocket. A second pocket was added in 1902. She said: 'Perhaps the most important reason why Levi's bought these jeans is that the company lost everything in the 1906 San Francisco earthquake and the first 50 years of our history was destroyed.'

**5** Now read these statements about the text and say whether they are true or false.

**a** There are no other jeans as old as these.

**b** Seth Weisser paid $10,000 for the jeans.

**c** Lynn Downey is an employee of Levi's.

**d** The jeans are made completely of one material.

**e** The jeans have fewer pockets than ones made after 1902.

**f** The Levi's company is more than 100 years old.

**6** Underline the four superlative forms in the text.

**7** Find words in the text that mean the same as a–f.

**a** too much ...........................................................

**b** common ...........................................................

**c** suitably ...........................................................

**d** pleased ...........................................................

**e** worn out ...........................................................

**f** surprisingly ...........................................................

# Grammar

## Comparison

**8** Make sentences using a comparative adjective and any other words needed. An example is given.

**a** Cotton shirts/cheap/woollen ones.
*Cotton shirts are cheaper than woollen ones.*

**b** Flat shoes/comfortable/high-heeled ones.

**c** Jeans/casual/trousers.

**d** Supermodels/thin/other people.

**e** Lily Cole/young/Kate Moss.

**f** New York/big/San Francisco.

**g** Jogging/dangerous/bungee-jumping.

**h** Clubbing/tiring/studying.

**9** Rewrite the following sentences using the structure *not as … as* and the word in bold.

**a** Last year the prices in this shop were lower.
**CHEAP**
This year the prices in this shop are
........................................................... last year.

**b** I think this exercise is easy.
**DIFFICULT**
This exercise is ........................................................... I thought.

**c** Ben won the race but George came second.
**FAST**
George was ........................................................... Ben.

G→ Student's Book page 166

# The virtual world

## Listening

1  **1 02** You will hear five short extracts in which people are talking about computer games. For questions 1–5, choose from the list (A–H) the job of each person. Use the letters only once. There are three extra letters which you do not need to use.

| | |
|---|---|
| **A** soldier | Speaker 1 [ 1 ] |
| **B** software developer | Speaker 2 [ 2 ] |
| **C** sales manager | Speaker 3 [ 3 ] |
| **D** psychologist | Speaker 4 [ 4 ] |
| **E** graphic artist | Speaker 5 [ 5 ] |
| **F** sportsperson | |
| **G** teacher | |
| **H** nanny* | |

\* someone whose job is to look after a family's children while their parents are at work

## Reading

2  Skim this text about two children, Harry and George. Do they prefer computer games or board games?

3  Scan the text for words or phrases that mean the same as a–h.

a  company ............................................................................

b  enjoy ..................................................................................

c  breaking off .....................................................................

d  finding solutions ............................................................

e  luck ....................................................................................

f  restrict ..............................................................................

g  enthusiastic .....................................................................

h  put ......................................................................................

Richard and Vicky Sabotowski try to work hard at their design business, as well as spend time with their two young sons. As games lovers themselves, the couple have found a way to make the most of their time at home. 'We always appreciate playing games as a family,' said Vicky, briefly interrupting an exciting but tense game of *Monopoly*. 'The children – Harry, 5, and George, 9 – really like games such as *Connect 4* and *Guess Who?*, which involve working out problems. Because these are games of chance, the cleverest people don't always win – and the children love beating us!'

The children both have computer games, but Vicky believes they find board games more fun. 'We try to limit how often they play on the computer because there's no social interaction. When they do play they get bored easily, but if we suggest a game of something like *Connect 4* they are always keen. To me, computer games are a bit of a cop-out – something to plonk your child in front of while you go and do something else.'

George agreed. 'With computer games you play them on your own and they get really boring. I much prefer playing board games.'

# Grammar

## Review of present tenses

**4** Match the sentence halves a–e and 1–5. Then fill each gap with a suitable verb in the present simple or present continuous.

    **a** A report published this week ..........................................

    **b** Parents ................................................ that many board games

    **c** According to a lot of parents, children .................................................. too much time in front of the TV,

    **d** More and more parents .................................................. their children from going outside to play

    **e** Board games .................................................. to be particularly attractive,

    **1** .................................................. educational and social benefits to their children.

    **2** as they .................................................. the whole family in an enjoyable indoor activity.

    **3** instead of playing outdoors, which .................................................. that they are less fit nowadays.

    **4** because they .................................................. it is dangerous.

    **5** that sales of board games .................................................. at present.

**5** Complete the email with verbs from the box in an appropriate form. Sometimes a verb can be used more than once. There is an example at the beginning (0).

| forget | hate | keep | know | like | realise |
|---|---|---|---|---|---|
| sound | suppose | understand | wish | | |

---

000                                   ◻

Delete  Reply  Reply All  Forward  Print

Dear Maya

How are you? I (**0**) ...*suppose*... you're working hard for your exams at the moment. I (**1**) ................................ I am! Although I normally (**2**) ................................ to do nothing in the evenings, this week the books are out every night! It's not easy to study, though. My little brother James (**3**) ................................ annoying me. He (**4**) ................................ I have to study but he (**5**) ................................ to be quiet. I (**6**) ................................ it most when he plays with his computer games. He (**7**) ................................ to turn up the volume and it (**8**) ................................ appalling! When I ask him to turn it down he never (**9**) ................................ why. Honestly, sometimes I almost (**10**) ................................ he wasn't my brother!

**G→** Student's Book page 167

# Vocabulary

**6** Complete this puzzle of words to do with games using the clues below. The correct number of letters is given to help you. What word appears vertically?

    **1** Computer games look great now because they have much better ................................ than five years ago.

    **2** An exact copy of something.

    **3** An ................................ is when you do something exciting.

    **4** Who you play against.

    **5** Companies often bring out a newer ................................ of the same game.

    **6** You use these when you are fighting.

    **7** To work out a puzzle or problem.

    **8** Games usually have very good sound ................................ .

```
1 _ _ _ _ _│_│_ _
2         _ _│_│_ _
3 _ _ _ _ _│_│_ _ _
4 _ _ _ _ _│_│_ _
5     _ _ _│_│_ _ _ _
6 _ _ _ _ _│_│_ _
7     _ _ _│_│_ _
8 _ _ _ _ _│_│_ _
```

**7** Choose the right adjective to describe the people in a–e. There is one extra adjective that you do not need to use.

| aggressive | anti-social | demanding |
|---|---|---|
| messy | mindless | sophisticated |

    **a** Brian turns up the volume on his sound system at 2 am and refuses to turn it down when the neighbours complain.

    **b** Kenny has piles of papers on the floor and leaves old coffee cups and chocolate wrappers on his desk for days.

    **c** Victoria is four years old and keeps asking her parents to play with her, even when they are trying to work.

    **d** Judy often gets angry and her boyfriend says she can be violent.

    **e** Claude wears Armani suits and goes to the best nightclubs in town.

# 3 Going places

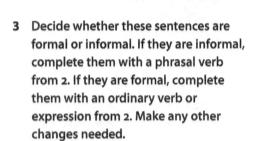

## Vocabulary

### Travel quiz

1 **Complete the following sentences with a suitable word. The correct number of letters is given to help you.**

a I'd really like to go on a _ _ _ _ _ _ round the Greek islands.

b The historic town centre was full of _ _ _ _ _ _ _ _ carrying guidebooks and cameras.

c We took the _ _ _ _ _ from Dover to Calais instead of the train through the tunnel.

d The _ _ _ _ _ we borrowed on holiday had red sails and enough space for two people.

e I think _ _ _ _ _ _ are more comfortable than campsites.

f There were quite a few boats sheltering in the _ _ _ _ _ _ _ _ .

g On a ship, you sleep in a _ _ _ _ _ _ .

h The _ _ _ _ _ _  _ _ _ _ _ made all the arrangements for our holiday.

i Tomas took the early _ _ _ _ _ _ and landed in Paris around 10.00 am.

### Phrasal verbs

2 **Informal phrasal verbs often have a more formal equivalent. Match phrasal verbs in 1–8 with the more formal alternative verbs a–h.**

| | |
|---|---|
| 1 to **come across** a person | a to be in the mood for |
| 2 to **get over** an illness | b to tolerate |
| 3 to **put up with** a situation | c to manage to see (a person or a place but not clearly) |
| 4 to **ring up** a person | d to leave/depart for |
| 5 to **keep on** doing something | e to telephone |
| 6 to **feel like** doing something | f to recover from |
| 7 to **make out** a person/thing | g to meet accidentally |
| 8 to **set off** for a place | h to continue |

3 **Decide whether these sentences are formal or informal. If they are informal, complete them with a phrasal verb from 2. If they are formal, complete them with an ordinary verb or expression from 2. Make any other changes needed.**

a I don't always ........................... making dinner in the evening so I often get a takeaway.

b Coaches ........................... Manchester every hour, on a daily basis.

c I don't know why you ........................... your boyfriend – he behaves like an idiot.

d Don't forget to ........................... Steve to remind him to bring some glasses to the party.

e We were informed that the company chairman was ........................... influenza, and was therefore unable to attend the meeting.

f If you ........................... to park your car outside my house, I'll have to consider taking legal action.

**4** Decide which of the following are written and which are spoken forms of English, and whether they are formal or informal.

Look at this example from the Student's Book:

*You don't have to socialise if you don't want to.*
ANSWER: *Informal, spoken English.*

**a** This compartment is reserved for non-smokers. ................................................

**b** John rang. Please ring him back sometime tonight. Steve ................................................

**c** We would be delighted if you could attend our son's wedding on 16th June.

................................................

**d** I wonder if you'd mind very much if I opened the window? ................................................

**e** You must be joking! ................................................

**f** Can I help you, sir? ................................................

**g** Out of order. ................................................

**h** Please give my love to your family. Best wishes, Liz ................................................

**i** Can you give me a hand with my things?

................................................

**j** OK, I'll be with you in a second.

................................................

# Grammar

## Obligation, necessity and permission

**5** Complete the following sentences with verbs from the box in a suitable form.

> have to   let   must   need   permit

**a** In Britain you ........................... drive on the left.

**b** In some countries you ........................... be 21 in order to drink in a bar.

**c** I'm going to stay in bed tomorrow morning as I ........................... go to work.

**d** 'I really think you ........................... to get your hair cut,' said Elizabeth's mother.

**e** My sister didn't ........................... me borrow her clothes when we were teenagers.

**f** Peter ........................... get the bus home last night as the trains were on strike.

**g** You ........................... have bought me a new watch for my birthday. My old one works perfectly well.

**h** Smoking ........................... in government offices any more.

 → Student's Book page 167

## Prepositions of location

**6** Complete the blog with suitable prepositions.

Home I New blog I Services I Travel

### My favourite place

This has got to be Sipadan, a coral island
**(1)** ..................................... the east coast of Borneo. I stayed
**(2)** ..................................... a little room with just a bed and a
wardrobe, nothing **(3)** ..................................... the walls or
floors. It was very simple – everyone ate together
**(4)** ..................................... the terrace at the front of the
building. Just **(5)** ..................................... the road from the hotel
is the beach, which is beautiful. You can walk
**(6)** ..................................... the island in about half an hour
although there are very strict rules about walking
**(7)** ..................................... certain parts of the beach at
night because the turtles lay their eggs in the sand.
Sipadan has some of the most amazing diving
**(8)** ..................................... the world. You can walk out to sea
and after 200 metres you come **(9)** .....................................
a coral wall which drops a kilometre straight down
**(10)** ..................................... the ocean floor.

## Reading

**1** You are going to read an article about a zoo in the United States. Read the article quickly to get an idea of what it is about and then answer these questions. Don't worry too much about any words that you don't know.

   **a** Where do northern white rhinos normally live?

   **b** Where is the Scripps Research Institute?

   **c** Which animal has the research team had a success with?

   **d** How many deep-freeze tanks are at the Frozen Zoo?

   **e** How many northern white rhinos are still living?

### Guessing unknown words

**2** In lines 14–17 of the article it says:

*They would be living specimens of one of the most endangered species on Earth, who after a few months would be trotting into wildlife parks …*

You might never have seen *trotting* before, but you can probably make a guess as to its meaning if you think about what other words might also fit there – for example, *walking, moving, going, running*, etc.

# The Frozen Zoo

*San Diego Zoo began collecting skin samples from rare animals in 1972 in the hope they might be used to protect these endangered species in the future. Paul Harris reports.*

The inside of a metal box filled with liquid nitrogen and frozen to –173°C (–280°F) is hardly the ideal habitat for a large African mammal. But, as a test tube is taken out of the container amid a cloud of white gas, a note written on its side can be seen. 'This is a northern white rhino,' says research scientist Inbar Ben-Nun as she reads out the label.

Ben-Nun is holding no ordinary scientific sample. For the frozen cells in that test tube could one day give rise to baby northern white rhinos and help save the species. They would be living specimens of one 15 of the most endangered species on Earth, who after a few months would be trotting into wildlife parks, and maybe, just maybe, helping repopulate their kind on the African grasslands. No wonder that the place where the sample came from is called the Frozen Zoo.

The Frozen Zoo was founded in 1972 at San Diego Zoo's Institute for Conservation Research as a place to keep samples of 25 skin from rare and endangered species. At the time that the first samples were collected and put into deep freeze it was not really known how they would be used and genetic technology was in its infancy. But there was a sense that one day some unknown scientific advance might make use of them. Now, thanks to a team at the nearby Scripps Research Institute, that day has come a lot closer.

35 Genetic scientists at Scripps, working from a business park in San Diego's northern suburbs, have succeeded in taking samples of skin cells from the Frozen Zoo and turning them into a culture of special cells known as stem cells and these could be used to bring to life long-dead animals whose species are almost extinct. The breakthrough, so far, has come with creating stem cells for the silver-maned drill monkey, Africa's most 45 endangered monkey.

'The Frozen Zoo was a wonderful idea,' says Dr Jeanne Loring, who is leading the Scripps team of which Ben-Nun is a part. 'This is the first time that there has been something that we can do. If we could use animals that were already dead to generate sperm and eggs, then we can use those individuals to create greater genetic diversity,' Loring says.

Loring's lab at Scripps holds samples from 55 the northern white rhino and the drill monkey, but the real Frozen Zoo, headed by Dr Oliver Ryder, just a few miles away, is on a much larger scale. Housed in a building inside San Diego Zoo, its freezers contain samples from 8,400 animals, representing more than 800 species. They include Gobi bears, endangered cattle breeds such as gaurs and bantengs, mountain gorillas, pandas, a California grey whale and 65 condors. The entire gigantic collection is in four deep-freeze tanks.

When it comes to species still on the brink, Ryder is insistent that we have a duty to save them and that the Frozen Zoo can play an important role. Especially close to Ryder's heart is one of the species that Loring is working on: the northern white rhino. There are just eight of the animals left alive on Earth. To put it bluntly: the 75 northern white rhino's gene pool is more accurately a rapidly drying-up gene puddle. But, if Loring's work succeeds in creating northern white rhino stem cells and then turning them into sperm and eggs, that gene pool can be deepened again.

Ryder makes no secret of how emotionally attached he is to saving the northern white rhino while there are still living animals, rather than just reviving some later entirely 85 from a test tube. He recalls witnessing the birth of a female northern white rhino more than 20 years ago and watching it being introduced to its herd. 'I saw her meet the rest of the rhino herd. There was a clear sense of how to meet the baby. If we wait until there are no white rhinos and then one is created from a test tube, to whom are we going to introduce it?' he says.

**3** Decide what these words from the article mean. You don't need to know exactly – just get an idea of the meaning. There are some clues in brackets to help you.

**a** to repopulate (what is *population*?) (line 18) ...............................
**b** infancy (what is *an infant*?) (line 29) ...............................
**c** extinct (line 42) ...............................
**d** breakthrough (think of the word as *break* and *through*) (line 42) ...............................
**e** to generate (line 52) ...............................
**f** housed (from *house*) (line 59) ...............................
**g** tanks (what do you put in a *petrol tank*?) (line 67) ...............................
**h** brink (what is the *brink of destruction*?) (line 68) ...............................
**i** puddle (the word it is compared with is *pool* – what is a *pool*?) (line 77) ...............................
**j** witnessing (what is a *witness*?) (line 86) ...............................

# Listening

**4** **1 03** You will hear a zoo keeper called Helena Tomkins, talking about her work. For questions 1–10, complete the sentences with a word or short phrase.

**Working in a zoo**

Helena was always keen on looking at **(1)** ............................... when she was young.

The subject Helena studied at university was **(2)** ............................... .

Helena currently looks after the **(3)** ............................... at her zoo.

Helena doesn't enjoy working in the **(4)** ............................... .

Helena's job in the morning is to prepare the **(5)** ............................... for the animals.

In summer, Helena gives **(6)** ............................... to the visitors twice a week.

Helena once had her **(7)** ............................... bitten by an animal.

Helena says that keepers need to carry a **(8)** ............................... with them at work.

Helena sometimes finds that some **(9)** ............................... who visit the zoo can be quite annoying.

Helena is hoping to visit **(10)** ............................... in the near future.

# Grammar

## *as* and *like*

**5** Decide whether to use *as* or *like* in the following sentences.

**a** He can't ride a horse ............................... well ............................... I can.
**b** Susanna prefers activity holidays ............................... sailing or walking.
**c** Your sister looks ............................... you.
**d** I came to school the same way today ............................... I did last week.
**e** He dressed up ............................... a policeman for the party.
**f** She used to work at the university ............................... a zoology lecturer.
**g** I enjoy going camping when it's warm, ............................... in July.

**G → Student's Book page 167**

## Compound adjectives

**6** Match the adjectives in the first column with those in the second column.

**a** duty-    catering
**b** cross-    free
**c** long-    handed
**d** absent-    minded
**e** hand-    distance
**f** first-    made
**g** second-    hand
**h** self-    class
**i** right-    eyed

**7** Which of the compound adjectives above collocate with the following nouns?

**a** a/an ............................... leather bag
**b** a/an ............................... journey
**c** a/an ............................... car
**d** a/an ............................... person
**e** a/an ............................... bottle of perfume
**f** a/an ............................... ticket
**g** a/an ............................... holiday

## Vocabulary

1 Complete the letter of complaint with words from the box. There are three extra words you do not need to use.

> compensation   conditions
> delighted   disaster   dreadful
> earlier   impossible   meant
> next   opposite   refund   spend
> stiff   surprised   thought   worse
> worried   unhelpful

## Grammar

### Review of past tenses

2 Complete this table of past tense forms. It includes both regular and irregular verbs.

| Infinitive | Past tense | Past participle |
|---|---|---|
| blow | *blew* | *blown* |
| find | | |
| grab | | |
| hold | | |
| keep | | |
| realise | | |
| shake | | |
| sink | | |
| try | | |
| wave | | |

Dear Sir,

My wife and I took an Ocean Cruise holiday with you last month, which was a **(1)** ............................ . I am therefore writing to ask for **(2)** ............................ .

Firstly, the food was **(3)** ............................ . In fact, my wife fell ill the day after we set off. We believe this was because of the breakfast she had eaten on board **(4)** ............................ that day. Her health got **(5)** ............................ during the trip but the ship's doctor was very **(6)** ............................ . I was quite **(7)** ............................ and this ruined the trip for me.

Secondly, our cabin was in an extremely noisy part of the ship, as it was **(8)** ............................ the disco. As my wife lay sick in bed, she was **(9)** ............................ more than once by drunken dancers who **(10)** ............................ our cabin was the nearest toilet. In the end, my wife locked the door. This **(11)** ............................ that I could not get into my own cabin late one evening and had to **(12)** ............................ the night in the bar.

Last but not least, your brochure promised 'excellent sailing **(13)** ............................'. However, for three days, there was a heavy storm and the ship rolled badly. My wife was scared **(14)** ............................ and even I found it unpleasant.

I demand a full **(15)** ............................ of the cost of the trip at your earliest convenience.

Yours faithfully,
K. Grumpington-Smythe
(Admiral)

3 Fill the gaps using the verbs in brackets in the correct tense.

> When Harry **(1)** ............................ (see) the cliff ahead of him, he **(2)** ............................ (know) that he **(3)** ............................ (take) the wrong road. He **(4)** ............................ (try) to stop the car but nothing **(5)** ............................ (happen). He **(6)** ............................ (go) rigid with fear as he **(7)** ............................ (realise) that someone **(8)** ............................ (interfere) with the brakes ...

Now choose one of these three endings to complete the story. Look up any words you don't understand in your dictionary. Write out the final sentences in full, adding suitable words of your own.

a cliff was getting nearer and nearer/threw himself out of window/car went over cliff

b swerved into field on left/noticed largest pile of hay ever/drove into haystack/survived

c went to pieces/screaming and shouting/car went over cliff/landed 200 metres below/burst into flames/Harry?

G→ Student's Book page 168

# Reading

4　Look at questions 1–10. Then read the six short texts (A–F) and answer the questions. The people may be chosen more than once.

**Which person**

| | |
|---|---|
| forgot to follow a safety measure? | 1 ☐ |
| describes a misunderstanding? | 2 ☐ |
| spent a night worrying about a relative? | 3 ☐ |
| believes they are lucky to be alive? | 4 ☐ |
| witnessed the theft of something valuable? | 5 ☐ |
| describes an incident underground? | 6 ☐ |
| looked after someone who was injured? | 7 ☐ |
| found employment during their trip? | 8 ☐ |
| describes their lack of fear? | 9 ☐ |
| wanted to take up something new? | 10 ☐ |

## A　Steffi

A group of us went to Germany two years ago. One afternoon, we had been to a lake to swim and we were strolling back to the tent through the forest. It went quite dark but it wasn't raining. Suddenly there was a flash of light and this enormous tree just to the right in front of us shook violently and started to fall in our direction. We turned and fled in absolute panic. It was a narrow escape. Jenny had dropped her bag. When we went back to find it, it was squashed flat underneath the tree trunk. That could so easily have been us!

## B　Annie

It was just before midnight when the doorbell rang. My dad answered and there was a policeman standing there. He said he had some bad news and asked to come in. He told us that my brother was trapped inside a cave up in Yorkshire with a friend of his. There had been some really heavy rain and the cave was in danger of flooding. He said there was 'little hope' of finding either of them alive. None of us slept at all, waiting for the phone to ring. However, when it did, it was my brother! He said they had found another way out and had spent the last two hours having a really good breakfast.

## C　John

We were driving along this mountain road, miles from anywhere, when we came across a trail of tins of food along the road. I looked out of the car window and noticed this camper van about ten metres below us in a field, with its back door hanging off. It had obviously swerved off the road. We stopped the car. A young man was climbing back up towards the road. He was covered in blood, so we offered to take him to hospital. As we drove off, with him lying on the back seat, he started asking about his girlfriend — was she all right? When we reached the hospital we found that someone else had picked her up and had taken her to casualty. Luckily, she was okay, and so was he — eventually — although he was kept in for ten days. They said they were travelling overland to India.

## D　Rosa

My friend Lauren and I were travelling in Australia. We'd both finished school that summer and were having a year off before university. We were able to find casual work as we moved around the country, doing waitressing mainly. We ended up in this tiny resort on the West coast, where they had a diving school. That was my choice because I'd always wanted to learn. Anyway, there we were, miles from anywhere, and working in the diving school office was my best friend from primary school! We had lost touch when we were eight as they had moved away, to Australia as it turned out. It was absolutely fantastic catching up with her.

## E　James

A funny thing happened to my mother when she was in Sweden on a lecture tour for work. She was travelling around, checking into a new hotel every evening. Someone came to meet her each morning, and in one place she was just checking out when they turned up. It was all a bit of a rush apparently. This person picked up a briefcase, thinking it was my mum's, and off they went. Much later, after the lecture, the person said, 'Don't forget your briefcase!' But of course it wasn't my mum's! In fact, she'd thought it belonged to the person meeting her! Fortunately, they found a contact phone number inside. The poor guy was very relieved when they called him and explained the mix-up!

## F　Helen

I was on a business trip in a big city and staying in a luxury hotel. When I'd checked in, the people on reception had warned me to lock my door at night, but this one particular night it had completely slipped my mind. I still remember waking up in bed and seeing this figure in black standing over me, with all my jewellery in his hands. The strange thing is that I wasn't frightened at the time. Thankfully, he didn't notice I was awake, so I closed my eyes again and lay absolutely still, calmly waiting for him to leave. When he did, I phoned the emergency hotel number immediately, but they never caught anyone.

# 6 What if?

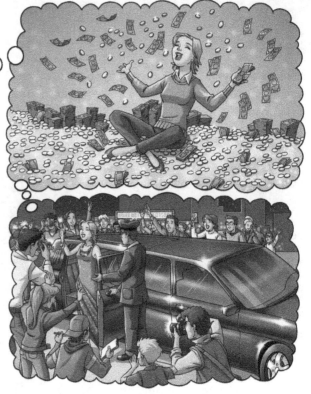

## Listening

1  **1.04** You will hear people talking in six different situations. For questions 1–6, choose the best answer (A, B or C).

1  You hear a man telling a woman about a new musical. What impressed him most?
   A the main performers
   B the storyline
   C the music

2  You hear a woman talking about a hotel. What disappointed her about it?
   A the prices that are charged there
   B the reality that only celebrities stay there
   C the fact that something was not genuine there

3  You hear a girl and a boy talking about being famous. What does the girl think would be difficult?
   A having too much money
   B being followed everywhere
   C treating friends differently

4  You hear an interview about swimwear. Where is the interview taking place?
   A in a clothes shop
   B at an exhibition
   C on a beach

5  You hear a woman talking on the phone. What sort of person is she?
   A unhappy
   B impractical
   C disloyal

6  You overhear a man calling a hotel. He wants to
   A alter a room reservation.
   B cancel a booking for dinner.
   C enquire about a special offer.

## Grammar

### Conditionals with *if* and *unless*

2  Complete the following conditional sentences with the correct form of the verb in brackets.

a  If he ............................................... (buy) a lottery ticket that morning, his life wouldn't have changed.

b  Unless someone ............................................. (claim) the prize by 11 pm, the money will be put into the good causes fund.

c  Would you talk to the press if they ............................................. (offer) you £10,000?

d  If anyone ............................................. (phone), say I'll be back at ten thirty.

e  Would you mind if we just ................................................. (grab) a sandwich for lunch?

f  If you ............................................. (be) so hard on her, she wouldn't have burst into tears like that.

g  I'd suggest meeting up with Danny tonight if he ............................................. (be) so unreliable.

h  I wouldn't be surprised if we ............................................. (end up) in a ditch, the way you're driving!

**G → Student's Book page 168**

**3** Put these adverbs of frequency in the correct place in each sentence.

 a Lottery winners find it difficult to sleep after they have heard the news. (usually)

 b I have time to read long novels these days. (rarely)

 c People are telling me to stop working so hard. (always)

 d Before the storm, I worried about those trees near the house. (never)

 e Now, if it's windy, I'm worried that they'll fall on us. (often)

 f What's happened to John? He's here by this time. (normally)

**4** Complete the second sentence so that it has a similar meaning to the first sentence, using the word given. Do not change the word given. You must use between two and five words, including the word given.

 1 Unless you leave now, you'll miss the train.
 **IF**
 You'll miss the train ............................................... now.

 2 If I'd known about the music competition, I'd have requested an audition.
 **IMPOSSIBLE**
 It was ................................................ an audition, as I didn't know about the music competition.

 3 Give me your address, as I might visit Barcelona.
 **CASE**
 Give me your address ................................................ visit Barcelona.

 4 I always watch the late-night news on TV.
 **NEVER**
 I ................................................ the late-night news on TV.

 5 George didn't get much sleep last night as usual.
 **HARDLY**
 Last night, George ................................................ as usual.

 6 Her parents were travelling in the desert so they couldn't follow the news.
 **KEEP**
 Her parents were travelling in the desert so they weren't ................................................ the news.

 7 The teen superstar still seems thrilled with her celebrity status.
 **ENJOY**
 The teen superstar still seems to ................................................ a celebrity.

 8 Wildlife above the Arctic Circle is endangered because of global warming.
 **IN**
 Wildlife above the Arctic Circle is ................................................ to global warming.

# Vocabulary

**5** Look at these sets of words. Which is the odd one out and why? Say what part of speech each set is.

 a celebrity   fame   talent   star

 b give   win   gain   receive

 c shock   misunderstanding   delight   panic

 d anxious   tense   irritated   nervous

 e deal with   look after   work out   keep away

 f generally   rarely   usually   normally

# Writing

**6** The words in these sentences are jumbled. Put them in the correct order and add punctuation. Sometimes there is more than one correct answer.

 a theatre I go often there isn't to town one my don't the very in because

 b use I phone could your please

 c lovely dress bought her a silk yesterday blue I

 d be keen never to Alan on swimming used

 e members few were a of students quite the audience

 f I eat Italian in would New York food I when lived

 g quietly watched pulled they down old cinema as crowd the the

 h asked money him the if man he give him some could

 i does not also bananas Alison only like she keen apples on is

 j been horrified life never I so my in have

# Life's too short

## Reading

1 You are going to read a newspaper article about a man who went diving in an ice-covered lake. Six sentences have been removed from the article. Choose from the sentences A–G the one which fits each gap (1–6). There is one extra sentence which you do not need to use.

# Ice Diving

**Nicholas Roe has a go at ice diving in the French Pyrenees.**

Right up to the moment when I plunge through the ice into the freezing waters of a mountain lake high in the French Pyrenees my day has been quite normal. I enjoyed breakfast at my hotel in the little ski resort of Saint-Lary. Then came a fine walk in the snow. What exactly made me book an ice-dive?

Driving to nearby Piau-Engaly along winding roads, I struggle for an answer, climbing eventually onto a snow-mobile for the final five-minute bounce across the ski slopes to the meeting place. **1 ⬚** Except for my guide, Nicolas Chapelle, who asks me if I really want to do this. Against my better judgement, I say, 'Yes'.

I pick up a big iron bar and help him make a hole in the ice. **2 ⬚** Deep in my stomach a bitter cold expands at the sight of that growing two-metre hole. Chapelle asks me to take off all my clothes, except for my underwear, and put on a big rubber suit. I feel a bit concerned. In theory, anyone can do this – divers, non-divers, even non-swimmers. Yet standing by that ice hole, it seems suddenly less easy.

I squeeze into the rubber gear like meat into a thick-skinned sausage, then put on the air tank, glancing over at ski runs full of bright figures rushing past. It's minus five out here, the water only seven degrees more.

Oh heavens. **3 ⬚** Chapelle says: 'Relax, but stay strong. You'll be fine.' Yes, but … oh, he's gone in.

Masked up and ready, his goggled-eyed face looking out above the lake surface, he signals me to follow. **4 ⬚** Water cold enough to kill if not for my suit. And it feels … ah, this curious sensation. I am not cold, not warm. I hover in the water, staring at the blue sunlight shining through the ice, lighting up the water.

Above me, the unbelievable roof of ice, marked now with a strange black fluid. **5 ⬚** But I feel free; amazed, too. I am contained by water, covered by thick ice in a clear space with fish swimming – I see them, they're right here – while in the distance a mountain stream runs into the farthest end of the lake. I feel as if I'm in space; as if I'm swimming in a huge building.

Chapelle won't let go of my air tank. **6 ⬚** However, it leaves me with a sense of annoyance because I want to twist and turn and enjoy this strange environment. Perhaps it's as well, then, that he steers me gently here, where I follow the fish for minutes; and here, where I stare back up at our escape hole and wonder at the blueness of the world.

Now we are heading back towards the light, breaking the surface where someone pulls me out. I am standing on ice, staring back into the water, barely able to believe that this is where I have been. And I can think about this for years. Which is, I now realise, why I came.

---

**A** The lake surface slowly breaks up into chunks big enough to fill a world-beating cold drink, the rim of black water growing with each smash.

**B** I find myself now sitting on the ice, staring in disbelief at my flippered feet hanging in the lake water.

**C** This turns out to be my own breath collecting in mobile puddles, trapped, as I am trapped.

**D** I pause occasionally on the way to watch the skiers go past the lake.

**E** There I find a fenced lake, a metal hut and nothing else.

**F** This is irritating but possibly safer.

**G** I'm afraid of looking afraid, so I plunge head-first, almost bashing Chapelle in the face, and together we sink, the water taking us down, down.

# Grammar

## Gerunds and infinitives 1

**2** Decide if the following sentences are correct. If not, make the necessary changes.

a Jenny suggested to go to the party in a taxi.

b I look forward to hear from you in the near future.

c I don't mind to do it.

d I'm interested learn Spanish.

e My brother wants to go to Japan.

f I'll help you with your homework when I finish to write my letter.

g I am used to do the washing-up.

h Let me make the tea.

i The children were made to get out of bed.

j I'm going to town for buy a new jumper.

k I object to pay to park my car.

l I can't afford to lending you any more money.

m My sister's too small to be a police officer.

**G → Student's Book page 169**

# Vocabulary

**3** Complete the following sentences by choosing the correct word.

a I don't think my team will ever *win / beat* the national championships – they are completely useless.

b The score at the end of the first half of the football match was 3– *zero / nil.*

c Some football players think the *referee / umpire* is an idiot.

d The basketball team has just had a new *pitch / court* built.

e I got my father a new set of golf *clubs / rackets* for his birthday.

f Most professional tennis players *give / take* up the sport when they reach their mid-thirties.

g The Formula 1 driver completed 30 *lengths / laps* of the track before he had to retire with engine trouble.

# Writing

**4** Read this report and add the necessary punctuation. You will need to put in CAPITAL LETTERS, full stops (.), commas (,) and apostrophes ('). You must also decide how many paragraphs and headings are needed.

report on the regional college football competition held on 3rd may venue this year the competition was held at highworth college this was an excellent choice of venue as there are six football pitches available all in excellent condition the competition all the teams in the competition were very experienced and played to a good level this provided excellent entertainment for the spectators the matches got off to a slow start mainly because of the bad weather it rained heavily throughout the morning but this cleared up after lunch then there were a few incidents where the referees decision was questioned but generally the matches were all played in a positive way with good team spirit the result the two finalists were chedbury manor college and fulbrook high the final score was 2–0 to chedbury and it was a good win for them their striker was particularly impressive and could perhaps even be considered for a professional club if he wanted to take that route all in all a very good days sport

**5** You have received this email from Kim, an English-speaking friend, who is coming to study at your college.

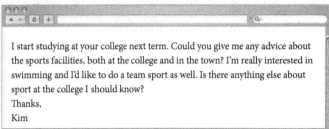

I start studying at your college next term. Could you give me any advice about the sports facilities, both at the college and in the town? I'm really interested in swimming and I'd like to do a team sport as well. Is there anything else about sport at the college I should know?
Thanks,
Kim

**Write your email in 140–190 words in an appropriate style.**

**Things to think about**

- Do you need any special vocabulary?
- Which facilities are you going to talk about – in general and in particular?
- What team sports are you going to mention?
- What are the instructors like?
- Anything extra you should add?
- Remember to punctuate your email!

# 8 Growing up

## Listening

1 **1 05** You will hear five short extracts in which people are talking about the job they wanted to do when they were young. For questions 1–5, choose from the list (A–H) what each speaker says. Use the letters only once. There are three extra letters which you do not need to use.

| | | |
|---|---|---|
| A chef | Speaker 1 | **1** |
| B teacher | Speaker 2 | **2** |
| C singer | Speaker 3 | **3** |
| D detective | Speaker 4 | **4** |
| E zoo keeper | Speaker 5 | **5** |
| F novelist | | |
| G astronaut | | |
| H psychologist | | |

## Vocabulary

### Verb collocations

2 Complete the following sentences with the correct form of the verbs from the box. Some verbs can be used more than once.

> break   do   have   keep   spend   taste

a My new car ............................................... 25 km to the litre.

b This cheese ............................................... a bit funny – when did you buy it?

c People always seem to ............................................... a fortune when they go on holiday.

d I ............................................... loads of camping holidays when I was young.

e I used to enjoy ............................................... time at my local zoo.

f His speech was so boring it was all I could do to ............................................... awake.

g My father said he would lend me his car at the weekend, but he ............................................... his promise.

### Adverb–adjective collocations

3 In the Reading text on page 54 of the Student's Book the writer describes her house as a 'perfectly hideous pink colour'. Which of the adverbs in A collocate with the adjectives in B?

**A**

highly        deeply        perfectly

**B**

praised     happy       disappointed     reasonable
amusing     ashamed     serious

Complete the following sentences using the correct collocation from above.

a John was ............................................... when he failed to win the motorbike race.

b Some people find his jokes ............................................... . Unfortunately, I don't.

c Although my hotel was rather expensive, I decided that the prices were ..............................................., considering the excellent service I received.

d I found it hard to believe, but my sister was ............................................... when she told me she was going to join the navy.

e His latest play has been ............................................... by the critics.

f I am ............................................... of my behaviour last night and am writing to you to apologise.

g I don't know why the baby started crying – he seemed ............................................... when I put him to bed.

## Definitions

**4** Match these words from the Reading text in the Student's Book with the definitions below.

| broom critical decent feast hideous landmark sensible |
| --- |

**a** A large amount of delicious food. .........................................................

**b** Something that tells you where you are. .........................................................

**c** Used to describe comments which are negative. .........................................................

**d** Good, worthy. .........................................................

**e** Used to describe someone who shows good judgement. .........................................................

**f** Used to describe someone or something which is very ugly. .........................................................

**g** Something you use to clean with. .........................................................

# Grammar

*used to* and *would*

**5** Read through the following article and decide which of the following would be suitable –
*used to, would* or the past simple. There is sometimes more than one possibility.

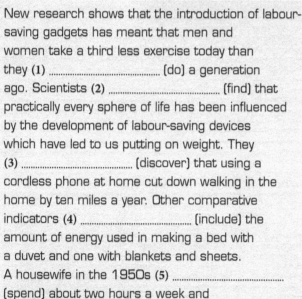

New research shows that the introduction of labour-saving gadgets has meant that men and women take a third less exercise today than they **(1)** ............................ (do) a generation ago. Scientists **(2)** ............................ (find) that practically every sphere of life has been influenced by the development of labour-saving devices which have led to us putting on weight. They **(3)** ............................ (discover) that using a cordless phone at home cut down walking in the home by ten miles a year. Other comparative indicators **(4)** ............................ (include) the amount of energy used in making a bed with a duvet and one with blankets and sheets. A housewife in the 1950s **(5)** ............................ (spend) about two hours a week and **(6)** ............................ (use) up 300 calories more than a person does nowadays.

Ernest Shaw, 69, **(7)** ............................ (confirm) how hard it **(8)** ............................ (be) to run a home in the 1950s. 'The jobs **(9)** ............................ (take) much more effort. The nearest shops **(10)** ............................ (be) a quarter of a mile away and my wife **(11)** ............................ (walk) there and back, laden down with heavy bags. There **(12)** ............................ (be) no supermarkets. You **(13)** ............................ (visit) the greengrocer, the dairy and the butcher.' The scientists **(14)** ............................ (estimate) that a shopper in the 1950s would have spent about ten hours and 2,300 calories a week walking from shop to shop.

**G** → Student's Book page 169

## Reading

**1** Read the article below, ignoring the missing sentences. How is the food industry failing shoppers?

# What do they really mean?

Food manufacturers and retailers have been letting shoppers down. This is the view of the CWS*, whose report looks at the language of food packaging.

According to the report, shoppers believe food labels because they think there are strict regulations in place. **1** ☐ So the food industry can get away with all sorts of cunning strategies to make products look bigger and sound better than they are.

The report has identified the different ways in which shoppers are misled. **2** ☐ Descriptions on packaging are sometimes inaccurate in an attempt to oversell the product. One example given in the report is the phrase 'haddock fillets', used for a product that is in fact cut from big blocks of fish rather than individual fillets.

**3** ☐ These include 'traditional', 'wholesome' or 'premium'. The claim that a brand is '90% fat-free'

hides the fact that it contains 10% fat, which is above recommended levels. Phrases such as 'free from preservatives' make a virtue out of a normal attribute of food.

Labels have a wide variety of text sizes on them. You sometimes need a magnifying glass to read the small print. **4** ☐

Another deliberate type of misinformation lies in the image. Many pictures on packets use small plates to make the product look bigger. **5** ☐

However, misleading messages on packaging could soon be a thing of the past. The CWS recently produced a code** which, if used, would end the current inaccuracies and half truths. **6** ☐ The minister for consumer affairs says the code 'will receive very serious consideration'.

\* Co-operative Wholesale Society

\*\* a set of rules

**2** Choose from the sentences A–G the one which fits each gap (1–6). There is one extra sentence which you do not need to use.

| | |
|---|---|
| **A** Meaningless adjectives are often used to give a positive message. | **D** By contrast, the hard sell information is given emphasis. |
| **B** It has called on the government to support it, as a way of improving food standards. | **E** The rules are, in reality, very weak at present. <br> **F** Photographs are sometimes retouched to achieve the same effect. |
| **C** This verdict has not pleased the food industry. | **G** The most common of these is poor labelling. |

**3** Find these words in the gapped article and sentences A–G.

   **a** four nouns to do with law    **b** three phrasal verbs

# Grammar

## Speculation and deduction

**4** Complete the following sentences with *must*, *might* or *could* (both are possible), *can't* or *couldn't* (both are sometimes possible).

**a** This ............................ possibly be the new Coca-Cola advert, though why on earth are they using polar bears?

**b** The ad for the Pentium chip ............................ be the best of the year. The way they manage to make a computer chip appear interesting is inspired!

**c** Here's an ad that shows a picture of 30 different puddings. It ............................ just be advertising desserts, surely?

**d** Do you remember that ad for a fizzy drink? It ............................ have been very successful, as they had to withdraw it almost immediately.

**e** Those ads for iPads ............................ be very successful. They've had so many hits on the internet!

**f** Product placement on TV shows ............................ be more effective than actual commercials. It depends on how many people are watching at the time, I suppose.

**G → Student's Book page 170**

**5** Complete the second sentence so that it has a similar meaning to the first sentence, using the word given. Do not change this word. You must use between two and five words, including the word given.

**1** I'm not sure, but I think a friend of mine did that voice-over for chewing gum.
**MIGHT**
That voice-over for chewing gum ............................ a friend of mine, but I'm not sure.

**2** Adam can't wait to go snowboarding next week.
**FORWARD**
Adam's really ............................ snowboarding next week.

**3** What is your uncle's job?
**FOR**
What ............................ a living?

**4** Before we start to plan the film shoot, we must agree the budget.
**DOWN**
Before we get ............................ the film shoot, we must agree the budget.

**5** I'm sure Rafael Nadal earned a lot for that car advert.
**BEEN**
Rafael Nadal ............................ a lot for that car advert.

**6** Their last commercial failed to convince viewers about the brand.
**MESSAGE**
Their last commercial didn't succeed ............................ across to viewers about the brand.

**7** The candidate couldn't register for the election because he missed the deadline.
**ABLE**
If the candidate hadn't missed the deadline, he ............................ register for the election.

**8** I was really impressed by the images in the advert.
**MADE**
The images in the advert really ............................ me.

# Vocabulary

## Collocations

**6** With which of the following words and phrases can you use the adjective *broad*? Which adjectives go with the remaining words and phrases? When you have decided, use a dictionary to study the different uses of these adjectives and *broad*.

**a** range of beliefs
**b** shoulders
**c** sigh
**d** Scottish accent
**e** smile of welcome
**f** feeling of guilt
**g** variety of products
**h** breath

**7** Complete the following definitions with words about advertising.

**a** A ............................ is a short song or tune used in TV commercials.

**b** A ............................ is a short phrase about a product that is easy to remember.

**c** The ............................ for a project is the amount of money available for it.

**d** A ............................ is a type of product made by a particular company.

## The final frontier

## Vocabulary

**1** For questions 1–8, read the article below and decide which answer (A, B, C or D) best fits each gap. There is an example at the beginning (0).

**Example:**

**0**   **A** predicting        **B** imagining        **C** believing        **D** intending

**Answer: A**

# Space tourism: we have lift-off

People are **(0)** ................ that space tourism could be a $700m industry by 2020. Thousands of paying passengers a year could be flown as far as zero gravity and back, for the most thrilling **(1)** ................ of their lives. Tickets are on sale now at a **(2)** ................ $200,000, from the billionaire Sir Richard Branson, whose Virgin Galactic company has big plans for its six-passenger spacecraft.

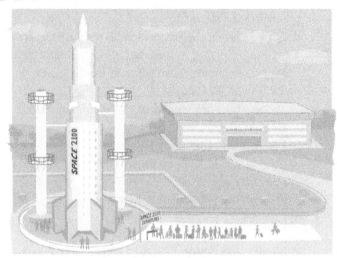

In the meantime, a growing **(3)** ................ of other business people are joining the space race, **(4)** ................ for the first time that there might actually be some money to be made. Virgin Galactic has already **(5)** ................ around $45m in deposits from people wanting to travel into sub-orbital space. Why are they so **(6)** ................ to do this? One common reason given is that people want to feel the **(7)** ................ of zero gravity, and many also say that they would like to **(8)** ................ the curve of the Earth from above.

| | | | |
|---|---|---|---|
| **1 A** lift | **B** sail | **C** flight | **D** drive |
| **2 A** pure | **B** mere | **C** bare | **D** pale |
| **3 A** amount | **B** sum | **C** figure | **D** number |
| **4 A** advised | **B** influenced | **C** convinced | **D** impressed |
| **5 A** taken | **B** kept | **C** borne | **D** held |
| **6 A** irresponsible | **B** impatient | **C** irritated | **D** impossible |
| **7 A** causes | **B** events | **C** issues | **D** effects |
| **8 A** view | **B** look | **C** gaze | **D** watch |

**2** Form a phrase with *at* to complete sentences a–f.

**a** ................................ I wasn't very interested in science fiction, but now I love it.

**b** George Clooney is ................................ in this film – the role is perfect for him.

**c** If you're in need of help, don't hesitate to call me ................................ , OK?

**d** Jessie knows a lot about space exploration – ................................ she says she does!

**e** The two countries have been ................................ for the last ten years but are ................................ willing to attend peace talks.

**f** Heavy rain over the last two days has raised the river level and puts the village ................................ of serious flooding.

# Listening

**3** **1 06** You will hear an interview with a science-fiction writer called Jed Stevens. For questions 1–7, choose the best answer (A, B or C).

**1** According to Jed, the best period of your life to start writing science fiction is
A in your teenage years.
B when retired from work.
C as a young adult.

**2** How did Jed become interested in science-fiction?
A by reading comics
B by watching television
C by listening to radio broadcasts

**3** What has proved especially useful to Jed's writing career?
A his background in computer programming
B his experience of living in different places
C his contacts in the scientific community

**4** Jed's first published work was
A a novel.
B an article.
C a set of short stories.

**5** What is the main attraction of writing science-fiction for Jed now?
A the ability to make a good living
B the opportunity to work on film versions
C the chance to explore new ideas about society

**6** According to Jed, how has science-fiction writing changed in the last 30 years?
A It has increased significantly in quality.
B Novels have been reduced in length.
C It is now based more on technology.

**7** Jed predicts that in 50 years' time,
A manned spacecraft will have travelled beyond the solar system.
B governments will have stopped investing in exploration.
C people will have been forced to find water elsewhere.

# Grammar

## Review of future tenses

**4** Make predictions about the future using these notes. Use the range of future structures covered in Unit 10. An example is given.

near future/scientists/work on moon.
*In the near future, scientists will be working on the moon.*

**a** 20 years/manned spacecraft/land on Mars.

..................................................................

**b** 22nd century/launch starships/destination/other galaxies.

..................................................................

**c** Soon/people travel to low orbit/Europe to New Zealand only an hour.

..................................................................

**Now write three more predictions of your own.**

..................................................................
..................................................................
..................................................................

**G →** Student's Book page 170

# Writing

**5** Read the advert below. Write a paragraph on this forthcoming event, using suitable future tenses and other words from this unit.

SPACE: THE FUTURE

**Conference at Elwood College of Technology, Melbourne, Australia**

10–12 January 2020

**Guest speakers:**
• science-fiction writer John T. Price
• leading scientist Professor Paul Rhodes

**Topics for discussion include:**
• beam-up technology
• moon settlements
• how to contact aliens

# Like mother, like daughter

## Vocabulary

Word formation

1   Read the short article below. Use the word given in capitals at the end of some of the lines to form a word that fits in the gap in the same line. There is an example at the beginning (0).

## How to find a partner

'Simply put, opposites don't attract, but similar types do,' says Dr Robin Russell of London University, who has spent a decade studying patterns of **(0)** __ATTRACTION__ . 'On average, the more similar you are to your partner **ATTRACT** in every way, from **(1)** ................... and obscure physiological factors like elbow **PERSON** shape, to attitudes and **(2)** ..................., amazing as it may seem the more you **APPEAR** are **(3)** ................... to get on.' **LIKE**

**(4)** ................... have any number of theories why. Early life might programme **SCIENCE** you to seek **(5)** ................... with people who look like your parents – and **RELATION** therefore look like you. Or you may make a random **(6)** ..................., but **CHOOSE** within the environment of your local **(7)** ................... network. **SOCIETY**

That said, there's a more than **(8)** ................... chance you will choose people **REASON** who look like you.

2   Put these adjectives into order of strength. If you think some are the same strength, put them together.

EXAMPLE: *(weak) upset    irritated    angry    furious (strong)*

| | | | |
|---|---|---|---|
| **a** uneasy | afraid | terrified | nervous |
| **b** thrilled | delighted | overjoyed | pleased |
| **c** depressed | disappointed | miserable | unhappy |

| | | | |
|---|---|---|---|
| **d** interested | obsessed | fascinated | eager |
| **e** speechless | surprised | astonished | shocked |
| **f** beautiful | attractive | stunning | lovely |

## American English

**3** In the Listening section in the Student's Book, there is an interview with an American called Hannah. She uses these words and phrases which are American English:

*on the subway …*
*she got real embarrassed …*

How would an English person say the phrases above in British English?

**4** Look at these other examples of American English and match them with the British English equivalents.

| American English | British English |
|---|---|
| 1 first floor | a sellotape |
| 2 fall | b motorway |
| 3 cookie | c lift |
| 4 trunk | d bank note |
| 5 vacation | e petrol |
| 6 freeway | f autumn |
| 7 gasoline | g ground floor |
| 8 apartment | h flat |
| 9 Scotch tape | i boot (of a car) |
| 10 elevator | j holiday |
| 11 bill | k biscuit |

# Writing

**5** Read through the following letter to a friend and correct it. There are 20 grammatical or spelling errors.

Dear Jody,

Thanks for your letter; it was good to here from you. You'll be pleased knowing that I've found someone to shair the flat with. She's called Elena Richmann and she's actress from Canada. I interviewed about 20 people before I seen her. She's very nicely and we really get on well together. Let me say you a bit about her. She's about 1m 50cm in hieght and has short, black, curly hair; in fact she look a bit like your sister! She's incredibly alive so she should be fun to have around. We're both interested at the same type of films and we seem to have similar tastes of music. She hates cook so I won't have to worrying about having a messy kitchen!

One drawback is that, when she has making a movie, she needs getting up really early, about 4.30 in the morning, to go to the set to get her make-up and costume sorted out. She says she'll be really quite, so we'll have to see. Anyway, I haven't noticed of any bad habits yet! You must to meet her – why don't you come over to the flat next Saterday and we can have a meal together? Drop me a line to let me know.

Love,

Tanya

**6** Look at these photos. A is a photo of your old neighbours and B is a photo of the people who have just moved in next door.

Now write a letter of between 140–190 words to a friend telling him/her about the new neighbours. Compare them with the neighbours you used to have and say which ones you prefer. You do not need to include postal addresses.

# 12 A great idea

## Reading

1 For questions 1–6, choose the answer (A, B, C or D) which you think fits best according to the text.

## Science flying in the face of gravity

It looked just like another aircraft from the outside. The pilot told his young passengers that it was built in 1964, a Boeing KC-135 refuelling tanker, based on the 707. But appearances were deceptive, and the 13 students from Europe and the USA who boarded the aircraft were in for the flight of their lives.

Inside, the area that normally had seats had become a long white tunnel. Heavily padded from floor to ceiling, it looked a bit like a lunatic asylum. There were almost no windows, but lights along the padded walls eerily illuminated it. Most of the seats had been taken out, apart from a few at the back, where the young scientists quickly took their places with a look of apprehension.

For 12 months, science students from across the continents had competed to win a place on the flight at the invitation of the European Space Agency. The challenge had been to suggest imaginative experiments to be conducted in weightless conditions.

For the next two hours the Boeing's flight resembled that of an enormous bird which had lost its reason, shooting upwards towards the heavens before hurtling towards Earth. The intention was to achieve weightlessness for a few seconds.

The aircraft took off smoothly enough, but any feelings that I and the young scientists had that we were on anything like a scheduled passenger service were quickly dismissed when the pilot put the plane into a 45-degree climb which lasted around 20 seconds. Then the engines cut out and we became weightless. Everything became confused, and left or right, up or down no longer had any meaning. After ten seconds of free-fall descent the pilot pulled the aircraft out of its nosedive. The return of gravity was less immediate than its loss, but was still sudden enough to ensure that some students came down with a bump.

Each time the pilot cut the engines and we became weightless, a new team conducted its experiment. First it was the Dutch, who wanted to discover why cats always land on their feet. Then it was the German team, who conducted a successful experiment on a traditional building method to see if it could be used for building a future space station. The Americans had an idea to create solar sails that could be used by satellites.

After two hours of going up and down in the plane doing experiments, the predominant feeling was one of exhilaration rather than nausea. Most of the students thought it was an unforgettable experience and one they would be keen to repeat. *39*

---

1 What does the writer say about the plane?
  A It had no seats.
  B The inside was painted white.
  C It had no windows.
  D The outside was misleading.

2 According to the writer, how did the young scientists feel at the beginning of the flight?
  A sick   B nervous   C keen   D impatient

3 What did the pilot do with the plane?
  A He quickly climbed and then stopped the engines.
  B He climbed and then made the plane fall slowly.
  C He took off normally and then cut the engines for 20 seconds.
  D He climbed and then made the plane turn over.

4 What was the point of being weightless?
  A To see what conditions are like in space.
  B To prepare the young scientists for future work in space.
  C To show the judges of the competition what they could do.
  D To allow the teams to try out their ideas.

5 What does 'it' in line 39 refer to?
  A the exhilaration
  B the trip
  C the plane
  D the opportunity

6 Why was this text written?
  A To encourage young people to take up science.
  B To show scientists what young people can do.
  C To report on a new scientific technique.
  D To describe the outcome of a scientific competition.

# Grammar

## The passive

**2** The *Cambridge English Corpus* shows us that exam candidates often make mistakes with the passive. Correct these sentences.

a  I had to been train by the manager.

b  Usually cuckoo clocks make out of wood.

c  The science exhibition will be visit by many people.

d  My camera stolen on the bus.

e  He was stolen his bike.

f  It has been prove that water freezes at 0 degrees C.

g  One speaks French here.

h  Many designs have make for new planes.

i  The house is painting at the moment.

j  The car cleaned now.

k  Maria born in April.

l  A jet flies by Hamid every day.

m  They were asking to a party.

n  Today's meeting has cancelled.

o  My house was building last year.

p  I hurt in a road accident.

**G → Student's Book page 171**

# Vocabulary

## Phrasal verbs with *come* and *take*

**3** Look at the context of the following phrasal verbs and decide on their meaning. Try not to use a dictionary until you have finished the exercise.

a  He **came into** a lot of money when his grandfather died.

b  She certainly **takes after** her mother – she's so tall.

c  He **took up** golf when he retired.

d  It took him two hours to **come round** after the blow to his head.

e  I'll be **taking over** the business when my father retires.

f  It was a problem we rarely **come up against**.

g  I didn't **take to** him at first, but now he's one of my best friends.

h  The Prime Minister didn't **come up with** any new ideas for tackling crime.

i  The information was too much to **take in** at first.

j  I **came across** an old letter in the attic the other day.

k  Her new job means that she will be **taking on** more responsibility.

# Listening

**4**  **1 07** You will hear a woman talking about a man called William, who built a windmill in his village in Africa. For questions 1–10, complete the sentences with a word or short phrase.

William's family didn't have the
(1) ..$................................ needed for him to stay at school.

William always wanted to get a job as a
(2) .......................................  .

William was able to spend some time in the
(3) .......................................  near his village.

William was keen to have electricity in his house so that he could have an electric (4) ...................................... in his room.

William's family wanted electricity so they could get (5) ........................................ more easily.

William's (6) ........................................ was the person who helped him build a windmill.

The basic structure of the windmill was made from an unwanted (7) .......................................  .

The blades of the windmill were made of
(8) .......................................  .

In William's village there is a (9) ...................................... which the villagers all have access to.

William's family is now able to grow
(10) ........................................ as well as maize.

## Reading

1   You are going to read an article about a teacher called Chris Searle. Read the first paragraph to find out more about him. Then skim the text, ignoring the missing sentences for the moment.

# Stepney Words

Chris Searle started teaching at Sir John Cass Secondary School in Stepney, East London, in 1970. This particular job had appealed to him partly because he knew the area. More importantly, he had done his postgraduate thesis on an East End poet, Isaac Rosenberg, and saw this part of London as 'a very poetical place'.

Searle had only just qualified but certain progressive ideas about education were already settling in his head. **1** Some of the governors and teachers were ex-army or had a church background; gowns were worn and canes were used to punish trouble-makers if necessary. Stepney was a poor area and the rest of the staff saw no hope for their pupils. However, to Chris Searle, these under-achieving teenagers were the 'sons and daughters of the poet Rosenberg' and poetry was the key that would unlock their potential.

**2** The short verses they wrote were sad and often bitter, with the East End shown as a place of no hope. To some of the staff at Sir John Cass, Searle's approach was alarming. Here was a teacher in his early twenties using the school as a laboratory for radical theories of education, and encouraging pupils to speak out. His classroom was noisy and lots of the girls had crushes on him. He saw pupils after school too, as he ran a half-price film club and lived in Stepney, unlike most of his fellow teachers, who fled each night to the suburbs.

Despite the negative attitudes of colleagues, Searle continued to focus on poetry. He persuaded a photographer, Ron McCormick, to bring his portraits of East London into class and with these visual images the poems got better and better. **3** The school governors, who thought these poems were too 'gloomy', had ordered Searle not to go ahead with the collection, but by March 1971, *Stepney Words* was out, paid for by Searle and parents. Extracts were even printed in the *Sun* newspaper.

Searle's 'enemies' (his own word) now made their move. One lunchtime in late May, the head called Searle in and fired him, instructing him not to come in after the end of the month. **4** Zeinaida de la Cruz, a strong-willed 16-year-old girl from Gibraltar, took charge: 'We arranged for people to tell each class. Immediately, everyone wanted to take action.'

When asked recently why they had all taken such a strong line on the sacking, she explained: 'It just didn't seem fair that a teacher everyone liked was being thrown out.' She remembers walking into the offices of a local newspaper after school to tell them what was going on. **5** Searle walked nervously to the school the next morning and found some 800 children standing outside the gates in the rain, where they stayed all day. Thanks to

Zeinaida, the journalists came along too. There was also a sympathy walk-out by the cleaning ladies, who made their feelings known by refusing to wipe the 'Don't sack Searle' graffiti off the school walls.

Other schools joined in and the next day there was a march to Trafalgar Square, in the centre of London. Searle stayed away, not wanting to be seen as their leader, but he did not let the matter rest from then on. **6** He also fought his dismissal through the union. In May 1973, the government's education secretary, Margaret Thatcher, ruled that Searle should be reinstated at the school. However, ignored by other staff and denied a class of his own, he decided to leave the school for good in July 1974. Searle continued to teach, however, and worked in many different countries around the world. He has also published his own poetry.

Lock up, unlock
That's me job for now
Lock up in the morning
Unlock at the end of day

It's an easy life
This job is
Just unlock in the morning
Enjoy meself all day

But at night, me back
It starts hurting
I can't bend
And turn that key

This job at night
It's not for me
In the daytime it's alright
But it's hard to turn
The key at night.

Christine Garratt

**2** Now choose from sentences A–G the one which fits each gap (1–6). There is one extra sentence which you do not need to use.

> **A** His class heard the news the same afternoon.
>
> **B** However, many pupils had seen their own parents on strike picket lines, so they did.
>
> **C** Searle contacted a local printer to arrange for their publication.
>
> **D** They called the national press, which transformed the protest into a major event.
>
> **E** These views were not shared by the school, which, although quite new, was run very traditionally.
>
> **F** Although banned from the school, he managed to publish a second *Stepney Words* later that year.
>
> **G** So he made them read it and write it, believing that in this way, his pupils would make sense of their lives and their surroundings.

# Grammar

## Reporting

**3** Here are some quotes from Chris Searle and his pupils, who were featured in a radio programme about *Stepney Words*. Rewrite them as reported speech. The first one is started for you.

**a** I went to the local paper and told them our plans. They asked me some questions to check me out, but in the end they promised to run the story. (Zeinaida)
*Zeinaida said that she had gone to the local paper …*

**b** That morning I went in through the side entrance. The school secretary was handing out the registers as normal, but there can't have been more than 20 or 30 kids in the whole building. (Chris Searle)

**c** While we were outside the gates, teachers came across and talked to us. Some were sympathetic, though they weren't able to admit it. Some were aggressive and threw gym shoes at us! (a pupil)

**d** Those children were made to feel that being ordinary meant failure. But it is the ordinary people and their daily work that make a country. (Chris Searle)

**G** → Student's Book page 171

# Vocabulary

**4** What do trouble-makers do? There are three other expressions with *make* in the article. Find them and look up their meanings in a dictionary. Then use the expressions and two from the box in the correct form to complete this short text about Chris Searle.

> make a start   make a good impression   make use of

> Chris Searle **(1)** .............................................. on his pupils, because he helped them to **(2)** .............................................. how they lived. To publish *Stepney Words*, he **(3)** .............................................. a local printer. The school governors did not approve of the book and soon after it came out, they **(4)** .............................................. and had him dismissed. Although Searle eventually got his job back at the school, the other teachers there **(5)** .............................................. to him and in the end he chose to leave the school.

**5** In these sentences written by exam candidates, use either a form of *make* or another verb collocation to complete the sentences.

**a** Our school is going to .............................................. improvements to its reception area.

**b** I .............................................. a very bad experience with tents while I was camping last year.

**c** Paul .............................................. up his mind to propose marriage to Mary.

**d** Finally, could you .............................................. me a favour?

**e** Technology has .............................................. my life easier.

**f** I don't need to .............................................. a diet or spend money in a gym.

**g** I believe that all parents should .............................................. the first step to .............................................. their children aware of the problems.

**h** Cycling is one of the best ways to .............................................. exercise.

**i** I really .............................................. myself at home.

**j** Saying goodbye always .............................................. me cry.

# 14 Career moves

## Vocabulary

### Word formation

1 Read the text below. Use the word given in capitals at the end of some of the lines to form a word that fits in the gap in the same line. There is an example at the beginning (0).

J ust imagine relaxing in your bath (0) ...*surrounded*... by a tropical **SURROUND**
beach scene. Or working in the kitchen alongside a wonderful
(1) .............................. of hand-painted fruits. These are just two **SELECT**
examples of the individually designed wall tiles that Jan and Barry
Harmer (2) .............................. in. They started their company, **SPECIAL**
*Tile Art*, because they felt there was a (3) .............................. gap **MASS**
in the market. 'There was limited (4) .............................. of **AVAILABLE**
good-quality English tiles,' explains Barry. Their designs are very
(5) .............................. and they are willing to take on some **IMAGINE**
unusual orders. One man turned up (6) .............................. with a **EXPECT**
picture of a JCB digger, wanting a mural of himself in the driver's seat
holding his new-born baby. The Harmers (7) .............................. **OBVIOUS**
enjoy running their small business from home and say they have no
plans for (8) .............................. . **EXPAND**

## Listening

2 **1 08** You will hear people talking in five different situations. For questions 1–5, choose the best answer (A, B or C).

1 You hear a man talking about his working life. What is his job now?
   A a journalist
   B a chef
   C a lawyer

2 You hear a conversation about getting a further qualification. What does the man say?
   A He wishes he could do his course part-time.
   B He believes he can support himself financially.
   C He hopes he will be able to get his old job back.

3 You hear a woman talking about her career. The woman chose her career in order to
   A travel to unusual places.
   B earn a decent salary.
   C work regular hours.

4 You hear two people at work discussing a colleague. The woman describes her colleague as
   A impatient.
   B irresponsible.
   C disorganised.

5 You hear a man talking about the skills needed for a new position in his department. What is the most important requirement for the job?
   A to have knowledge of a language other than English
   B to have experience of telephone selling
   C to have a qualification in maths

# Writing

**3** Read this news report about a young millionaire. Then use the information to give you an idea for the essay in 4 below.

Nick D'Aloisio's 'ridiculous' life (his word) is due to the immense popularity of the iPhone app he created. Called *Summly*, it allows you to process news more easily on a mobile device. Essentially, it pulls in news from a variety of sources and uses a computer algorithm to reduce it to a couple of key sentences, with users choosing the subjects most relevant to them.

Nick D'Aloisio, Britain's 17-year-old app developer

Nick set up a company to develop the app, though at 16 he was too young to be a director and so his mother had to take on that role. The company has just been bought by Yahoo for an estimated £18 million, changing Nick's life for good. Although he still plans to apply to university, his studies for school exams will now be reserved for evenings, as he has a new day job as a Yahoo employee, working out of their London offices.

He doesn't appear to feel under pressure from his overnight success, even though the media refer to him as 'the new Mark Zuckerberg' and therefore expect him to be a billionaire by his early 20s. He does however admit to being inspired by the Facebook biopic *The Social Network* and believes there is no upper limit to possible future success. "I was as low as you go, a kid with no experience, and I got to this position just through an idea. If the concept's good enough then it will work."

**4** Read the exam question and add your own idea to the notes.

In your English class you have been talking about starting a business. Now your English teacher has asked you to write an essay.

Write an essay using **all** the notes and give reasons for your point of view.

> Teenagers cannot succeed in business until they gain some experience. Do you agree?
>
> **Notes**
> Write about:
>
> 1. why teenagers start companies
> 2. how studying might be affected
> 3. ........................... (your own idea)

Write your essay in 140–190 words.

**5** Now read the sample answer, choosing the right word or phrase in 1–7.

> *Teenage success*
>
> This essay considers whether experience of the business world is needed in order to succeed. **(1) Therefore / Although** it is true that teenagers who are still at school may not have much awareness of working life, they can get advice from adults. **(2) So / Because** first-hand knowledge is not essential.
>
> Take the example of Nick D'Aloisio, who started his own company at 16. What was important **(3) in any case / in his case** was that he saw a good business idea and had enough understanding of mobile technology to develop it. **(4) In any case, / In that case,** his mother is a director in his company so probably helped him.
>
> **(5) On the one hand, / On the other hand,** it cannot be easy to cope with a business while at school. It may be necessary to put studying on hold. **(6) Again, / Secondly,** in D'Aloisio's case, he chose to study in the evening to keep his options open.
>
> **(7) To sum up, / In contrast,** it seems perfectly possible for teenagers to succeed if they have a solid concept to work with. It should be remembered that Mark Zuckerberg, the founder of Facebook, became a billionaire in his early 20s and others have achieved similar success.

# Grammar

## *all* and *the whole*

**6** Complete these sentences, which contain an expression with *all* or *the whole*.

a The best ........................... about my new job is that I don't have to drive into work any more.

b I'll be away from my desk for the ........................... next week, but you can email me if anything comes up.

c On ........................... , I really love where I work, because my colleagues are so nice.

d The salary and conditions are reasonable but above ........................... , it's the travel opportunities that have persuaded me to apply for this post.

e I'd been sitting at my computer most lunchtimes, too busy to leave the office, when ........................... sudden, I decided to quit.

**G → Student's Book page 172**

# Too many people?

## Vocabulary

**1** Read the following article about the environmental group Greenpeace and decide which answer (A, B, C or D) best fits each gap. There is an example at the beginning (0).

**Example:**

**0** **A** protect      **B** care      **C** look      **D** tend

Answer: A

### Greenpeace

Greenpeace is an independent organisation that campaigns to **(0)** ........ the environment. It has approximately 4.5 million members worldwide in 158 countries, 300,000 of these in the United Kingdom. **(1)** ........ in North America in 1971, it has since opened offices round the world. As well as its campaigning **(2)** ........ , it also has a charitable trust which **(3)** ........ scientific research and undertakes educational projects on environmental issues. Greenpeace **(4)** ........ in non-violent direct action. Activists draw public attention to serious threats to the environment. **(5)** ........ issues on which the organisation is campaigning include the atmosphere (global warming), the **(6)** ........ of the rainforests and toxic waste being emitted from factories. Greenpeace is committed to the principles of political independence and internationalism. By exposing **(7)** ........ to the environment and in working to **(8)** ........ solutions, Greenpeace is really helping to save the planet.

| | | | |
|---|---|---|---|
| **1 A** Built | **B** Formed | **C** Invented | **D** Produced |
| **2 A** work | **B** job | **C** occupation | **D** position |
| **3 A** pays | **B** funds | **C** rewards | **D** earns |
| **4 A** accepts | **B** depends | **C** holds | **D** believes |
| **5 A** Instant | **B** Current | **C** Immediate | **D** Next |
| **6 A** ruin | **B** extinction | **C** destruction | **D** downfall |
| **7 A** warnings | **B** threats | **C** promises | **D** difficulties |
| **8 A** find | **B** make | **C** set | **D** sort |

**2** Complete the sentences with words you have used in the Student's Book. The correct number of letters is given to help you.

**a** People put used glass and paper in separate containers so they can be _ _ _ _ _ _ _ _ _ .

**b** I hate people who drop _ _ _ _ _ _ _ .

**c** I can't afford a new car. I'll have to get a _ _ _ _ _ _ _ - _ _ _ _ one.

**d** Last year there was a _ _ _ _ _ _ _ because there wasn't enough water.

**e** This year there are _ _ _ _ _ _ _ because there has been too much rain.

**f** A _ _ _ _ _ of lightning lit up the sky, and then came the thunder.

**g** We got caught in a heavy _ _ _ _ _ _ and didn't have an umbrella with us.

**h** Chemicals and exhaust fumes are all _ _ _ _ _ _ _ _ _ _ of our planet.

**i** Coal and oil are known as _ _ _ _ _ _ _ _ _ _ _ _ .

# Writing

**3** You have recently had a letter from your penfriend, Susan, telling you about the area where she lives in Scotland. Complete the letter with words from the box below.

> although  as  as a result
> because  besides  despite
> furthermore  so  though
> when

**4** Now write your reply to Susan. Remember to use your English-English dictionary if necessary.

Think about:

- Location: in the north of, to the south of
- Size: an average-sized town, a small village, the capital city
- Climate: damp, humid, tropical, temperate, arid
- Landscape: mountainous, flat, hilly, forested, built-up
- Population activity: agricultural, industrial, academic, fishing

Dear ........................... ,

It was great to hear from you last week and to get all your news. We're all fine here and looking forward to the summer holidays. I thought in this letter that I'd tell you a little bit about Dunlochry, where I live.

**(1)** ........................... you know, I live in a very quiet area of Scotland, which is very close to the sea and completely free from pollution. **(2)** ........................... a small population of only 350 people, my village is quite busy, especially in the summer, **(3)** ........................... all the tourists come.

**(4)** ........................... the ferry to the islands, there is also the castle by the loch (like a lake), which is popular with visitors.

**(5)** ........................... as you can imagine, most people here work for the ferry company or in hotels and souvenir shops.

**(6)** ........................... Dunlochry is quite far north, it has a mild climate **(7)** ........................... of the Gulf Stream. One of my neighbours even has a palm tree in his garden! The landscape is very mountainous and **(8)** ........................... there is very little flat land available for farming. Sheep farming has been carried out here for centuries **(9)** ........................... and is quite profitable.

**(10)** ........................... , a large number of the local women make money in the winter from knitting the wool into sweaters.

That's all for now. Write and let me know something about where you live in your next letter.

Best wishes,
Susan

# Grammar

*some, any, no, every*

**5** *Some, any, no* and *every* can combine with *thing, body/one* and *where* to form a compound. Complete the following sentences using an appropriate form.

**a** Have you got ........................... I can read on the way home?

**b** Peter left without telling ........................... where he was going.

**c** She's really well travelled. She's been ........................... .

**d** ........................... told me that the trains were on strike – I had no idea at all!

**e** Surely we can do ........................... to make our streets safer.

**f** Believe me, he really does live five kilometres from ........................... .

**g** Ministers usually don't have ........................... to say when they are asked what they are doing to help the environment.

**h** ........................... I know is a non-smoker, so I don't need any ashtrays.

**i** The policeman told us that ........................... we said would be taken down and could be used in evidence against us.

**G →** Student's Book page 172

# Eat to live

## Reading

1 You are going to read about four women who are vegetarian. For questions 1–10, choose from the women (A–D). The women may be chosen more than once.

**Which woman**

| | |
|---|---|
| was influenced by someone? | **1** |
| is aware that she might not be eating a healthy diet? | **2** |
| has joined an organisation to find out more? | **3** |
| has enjoyed cooking for a long time? | **4** |
| checked with a specialist that being a vegetarian is healthy? | **5** |
| dislikes some vegetarian food? | **6** |
| is vegetarian for moral reasons? | **7** |
| had some problems at first? | **8** |
| suffers physically after eating meat? | **9** |
| lives with someone who doesn't completely agree with her? | **10** |

**B RACHEL**

Rachel has been a vegetarian for four months. 'It was my New Year's resolution,' she says. 'It's been a real eye-opener. I didn't realise that a lot of things I eat – like sauces – have meat products in them. I became a member of the Vegetarian Society to get more information. It's made me realise how much goes into our food and how little we consumers know. I eat lots of pasta and lentils because they are so cheap and easy to prepare. At first I put on a lot of weight because of all the cheese I was eating. Now I'm much better at experimenting with food and I'm enjoying cooking new things. I'm now trying to convince the other people in my flat to become vegetarian too.'

Having a vegetarian boyfriend at school led Chloe to think about giving up meat. Then she saw a TV programme about badly treated farm animals and it gave her the final push. 'I gave it up there and then,' she says. 'I did worry about my kids eating only vegetarian food, but my doctor says it's fine. As a family, we eat lots of fresh food, pasta and lentils, and try to eat organic food – although it's not always easy. I do use convenience food quite a bit as I work full-time. We don't often eat puddings and usually have fresh fruit after a meal. The children have the worst time because their friends tell them it's unhealthy to be vegetarian. However, the children are keen to stay vegetarian.'

**C CHLOE**

**A LUISA**

Luisa has been a vegetarian for four and a half years. She says, 'I've never really liked meat, and throughout my teens ate less and less of it. Then, I went abroad on holiday one year and when I came back I decided to give up meat for good. I'm more interested in food and cooking now than I used to be. My husband and I love food and we spend hours experimenting with different recipes – there's so much you can do with vegetarian food. Our favourite foods are mainly Italian and Indian. We probably eat too much fat in our diet and are aware that we need to cut down. We're not that keen on brown rice and lentils. I also hate things that try to imitate meat. I study labels carefully but we don't worry too much when we eat out.'

'I love vegetarian food and eat it at least four days a week, sometimes more,' says Kate. 'I prefer the taste, textures and flavours – there are so many interesting ingredients to choose from. I've never been a great meat eater, even as a child, but I haven't been persuaded to cut out meat entirely, as I love dishes like chicken curry and salmon. I've been a keen cook for years. Being vegetarian has made me more aware of my health. When I do eat meat, I feel sleepy and slow.'

**D KATE**

# Listening

2 **[1 09]** You will hear five short extracts in which people are talking about food. For questions 1–5, choose from the list (A–H) what each writer says. Use the letters only once. There are three extra letters which you do not need to use.

**A** I like to have a big breakfast.

**B** I see food as an important theme in my books.

**C** I like to eat while I'm writing.

**D** I see food as a reward.

**E** I'm quite careful about what I say about food in my books.

**F** I'm trying to cut down on what I eat.

**G** I prefer simple food.

**H** I put recipes into my novels.

| | | |
|---|---|---|
| Speaker 1 | | 1 |
| Speaker 2 | | 2 |
| Speaker 3 | | 3 |
| Speaker 4 | | 4 |
| Speaker 5 | | 5 |

# Grammar

## The article

3 **Fill the gaps in the following sentences with** *a, an, the* **or – (when no article is needed).**

**a** We went out for ...................... meal at ......................
restaurant where we first met.

**b** Why are ...................... potatoes so popular with
...................... British?

**c** We flew across ...................... Atlantic Ocean by
...................... Concorde to ...................... United States.

**d** ...................... apple ...................... day keeps ......................
doctor away, or so they say.

**e** I worked as ...................... waitress in ......................
summer before I went to ...................... university.

**f** I think ...................... coffee is ...................... best drink
in ...................... world.

**g** Susan was invited to ...................... dinner party at
...................... Jane's last week.

**h** When we go abroad we always bring back some
of ...................... food and ...................... drink that we
enjoyed.

**G → Student's Book page 172**

4 **The article below is about the American-Chinese chef Ken Hom. For questions 1–8, think of the word which best fits each gap. Use only one word in each gap. There is an example at the beginning (0).**

## Ken Hom

I started cooking in my uncle's Chinese restaurant **(0)** _AT_ the age of 11. At first, I just washed the dishes, then chopped and sliced the vegetables. But as soon **(1)** ...............
the chefs went out of the kitchen I'd try to copy the dishes I'd seen them cook. The first dish I attempted to make was fried rice. It's **(2)** ...............
difficult to mess up that anyone can cook it.

By the **(3)** ............... I was 15 I was fed **(4)** ............... with working 12-hour days in the restaurant. So, I **(5)** ...............
up my mind to go to university to study history of art and only started cooking again in **(6)** ............... to get some extra money.

My mission **(7)** ............... always been to encourage people to eat less fat and meat and more vegetables. Kids say they don't eat vegetables, but they usually haven't had them stir-fried. Cooked **(8)** ............... this they are delicious, healthy and fun.

# Collectors and creators

## Vocabulary

### Word formation

**1** Read this short article about unusual hobbies. Use the word given in capitals at the end of some of the lines to form a word that fits in the gap in the same line. There is an example at the beginning (0).

Playing tiddlywinks

An inn sign

Haggis hurling

# STRANGE PURSUITS

| | |
|---|---|
| Go through the Directory of British Associations and you'll find about 7,000 groups that are considered large enough to be of national **(0)** <u>IMPORTANCE</u> . That number swells to around 150,000 with the **(1)** ............................................... of every local gardening club, film society and special interest group, most providing a meeting place for like-minded people. | IMPORTANT<br>INCLUDE |
| With such an **(2)** ............................................... choice available, there must quite literally be something for everyone. Let's kick off with the Haggis* Hurling Association, which supervises what has become a Guinness Book of Records event (current record for a 680 gram haggis: 55 metres) and organises **(3)** ............................................... to raise money for good causes. | END<br><br><br><br>COMPETE |
| Then there's tiddlywinks, which has had an official association since 1958. Most people start playing tiddlywinks 'for a joke', but then they get hooked, perhaps because most of the post-match **(4)** ............................................... is done in the pub. | ANALYSE |
| If tiddlywinks strikes you as too **(5)** ............................................... , the leisurely study of pub signs might be more your cup of tea. The Inn Sign Society has 400 members who spend their time travelling the country in search of **(6)** ............................................... pub signs. Their founder used to have a **(7)** ............................................... of 300 actual signs, as well as 20,000 photos of pub signs, going back to the 1930s. | ENERGY<br><br>USUAL<br>COLLECT |
| To get the addresses of these clubs and others, why not visit your local library? **(8)** ............................................... try searching the internet. You're bound to find something appealing that you've never even thought of! | ALTERNATE |

\* A haggis is like a large, round sausage and is eaten in Scotland.

**2** Find words and phrases in the article in 1 that mean the same as a–f.

| | | |
|---|---|---|
| **a** grows | **c** best distance | **e** become addicted |
| **b** start | **d** charities | **f** certain |

**3** The article refers to *like-minded people*, meaning people with similar views. How many words with *like* in the box do you recognise? They have all appeared in previous units. Complete the sentences using each one once.

> like   likeable   likeness   liking   unlikely

**a** Goat-driving seems a very .................................. hobby to me, but there's an official club listed here!

**b** Dressing up in old clothes and fighting battles isn't to my .................................. .

**c** My nephew goes beach-combing for shells, unusual pebbles and things .................................. that.

**d** Once the full make-up has been put on, he shows an amazing .................................. to Captain Kirk.

**e** Gerry is a very .................................. 75-year-old, who enjoys nothing more than dancing to old rock music.

# Writing

**4** Write a paragraph on haggis hurling, using the rules below. Try to use relative clauses to make your sentences longer. For example:

*The Haggis Hurling Association, <u>which was founded in 1977 by Robin Dunseath</u>, challenges people to throw a haggis of a certain weight as far as they can.*

---

### Rules

**The haggis …**

- must be prepared according to the traditional recipe
- should be cooled at the time of hurling
- will be inspected for illegal firming agents such as cement
- must not break or split on landing (this results in disqualification)
- should weigh 500 grams (junior and middle-weight events) or up to 1 kg (heavyweight event)
- should have a maximum diameter of 18 cm and length of 22 cm (junior and middle-weight events).

# Grammar

**5** For questions 1–8, read the text below and think of the word which best fits each gap. Use only one word in each gap. There is an example at the beginning (0).

Elisabeth Daborn, **(0)** __WHO__ works as a teacher and artist, re-enacts history with her partner Kevin Cowley and their children. The adults spend most of their weekends fighting. However, **(1)** .......................... is nothing personal! They both belong **(2)** .......................... Regia Anglorum, one of Britain's two main Viking re-enactment societies. Elisabeth explains their shared passion. 'Kevin used to **(3)** .......................... keen on LARPing – Live Action Role Play – but after **(4)** .......................... while, he decided he wanted something more authentic. So he joined Regia, **(5)** .......................... specialism is the period 950 to 1066. I joined too, but because there's **(6)** .......................... proof that Viking women fought, I dress up as a man. Over the years, Regia's been in many TV series and in a rock video, **(7)** .......................... we had to row our longship and headbang at the same time. The longship, **(8)** .......................... was built for the film *Erik the Viking*, is safe to use on rivers, although I wouldn't like to go out to sea on it!'

# What's in a book?

## Reading

1 You are going to read a magazine article about the writer Daphne du Maurier. Six sentences have been removed from the article. Choose from the sentences A–G the one which fits each gap (1–6). There is one extra sentence which you do not need to use.

# Daphne du Maurier

*Often seen only as a writer of popular romances, Daphne du Maurier's work is much more complex than that. To mark the centenary of her birth this month, Patrick McGrath relishes the dark side of her short stories …*

Daphne du Maurier was born into a famous London theatrical family, but lived in Cornwall for most of her life, in a large romantic house near the sea called Menabilly. Although she never owned it, she adored living there and it was where she raised her family. There can be no doubt that Menabilly and its surroundings inspired several of her novels and short stories.

Du Maurier enjoyed early success as a writer and continued to have a wide readership throughout her career, with bestsellers such as *Jamaica Inn*, *The House on the Strand* and, of course, *Rebecca*. **1** [ ] He also adapted her spine-chilling short story *The Birds*, choosing to set it in northern California rather than in its originally wild Cornish location. Apparently, Daphne du Maurier hated this adaptation.

Before writing her collection of short stories *The Apple Tree*, to which *The Birds* belonged, du Maurier had been known for her romantic fiction. She had made her mark in particular with historical novels such as *Frenchman's Creek* and *Jamaica Inn*. However, *The Birds* was not inspired by the past. **2** [ ] Arguably, it was the starting point for an entire genre devoted to narratives about natural disaster.

*The Apple Tree* collection was published in 1952. **3** [ ] It is about a man in an unhappy marriage, whose wife Midge suddenly dies. Bizarrely, he starts to hate a particular apple tree in his garden, as he sees in it his dead wife's most irritating characteristics. He decides to get rid of it once and for all. Eventually the tree destroys him, and we understand that it is through his own bad feelings towards Midge that he has brought this end upon himself.

Nature in du Maurier's stories rarely has a favourable effect on humans, other than in the coming-of-age story called *The Pool*. This beautiful tale takes place in the middle of summer in the English countryside. By a woodland pool, a girl finds a 'secret world' – a strange underwater place with fantastic beings. **4** [ ] This is nature as it is experienced by a child: magical, enchanting and unreal. With the end of childhood, her secret world is out of reach for ever.

In a powerful story called *The Chamois*, we follow a husband and wife as they go up a mountain in northern Greece. The tensions in the marriage are quickly established, as is the man's obsession with hunting that elusive animal, the chamois. Having reached the top of a mountain pass, the couple are taken into the high regions by a shepherd. What follows in the story reveals the truth of each character's

nature, in a manner not unlike that of the Ernest Hemingway hunting story *The Short Happy Life of Francis Macomber*. **5** [ ] It is the actions of the woman that are especially surprising in du Maurier's tale, just as they are in the Hemingway one.

Daphne du Maurier wrote exciting plots, and was highly skilled at creating suspense. **6** [ ] Indeed, in her lifetime she published more than three dozen works of fiction, history and biography. A new edition of *Don't Look Now and Other Stories* has been published by the Folio Society.

---

**A** While the title story lacks the tension of *The Birds*, there are similarities in the treatment of nature.

**B** Not only this, she was also a writer of fearless originality.

**C** What she in fact discovers is the power of her own imagination.

**D** Alfred Hitchcock turned this wonderful tale into a memorable film of the same name.

**E** The bandages are removed and, to the woman's astonishment and horror, everyone she sees has the head of an animal.

**F** It seemed instead to look ahead to major environmental catastrophe in the near future.

**G** The climax of his story similarly involves a guide, a beast and a gun.

# Vocabulary

**2** Find 14 more words to do with books and writing in this wordsearch. Words can be horizontal or vertical.

| F | T | H | R | I | L | L | E | R | A | N | E |
|---|---|---|---|---|---|---|---|---|---|---|---|
| I | L | L | U | S | T | R | A | T | I | O | N |
| C | T | P | A | O | T | C | L | E | O | V | N |
| T | R | U | C | X | C | H | A | P | T | E | R |
| I | H | B | T | L | R | A | N | H | I | L | P |
| O | N | L | I | C | K | R | Y | T | U | I | L |
| N | B | I | O | G | R | A | P | H | Y | S | O |
| W | E | S | N | C | S | C | E | N | E | T | T |
| Y | O | H | R | A | O | T | T | F | T | N | L |
| K | E | E | H | L | M | E | V | E | N | T | A |
| X | O | R | A | M | I | R | E | V | I | E | W |
| W | E | S | T | O | R | Y | O | P | L | A | Y |

# Grammar

## enough, too, very, so, such

**3** Correct the following sentences.

a I have never read a such long book as this one.
b The story was very complicated that I gave up.
c Hardback books are too much expensive.
d Enough books weren't ordered.
e I was too sad to hear of the novelist's death.
f It was a such exciting plot.
g The print in this paperback isn't enough big.
h Characters as these are quite unusual.

**4** Complete the review with *so, such, too, very* or *enough*.

*The Old Man and the Sea* by Ernest Hemingway is
(1) ............ easy to read and it isn't (2) ............ long a book,
either. You may find the story (3) ............ compelling to put
down. On the (4) ............ first page, you learn that the old
man has gone 84 days without catching (5) ............ much as
a single fish.

On that opening page, almost everything about him is
described as old – characteristics (6) ............ as the wrinkles
on his neck and the many scars on his hands. Interestingly
(7) ............ , however, you are also told that his eyes are not
old; they are 'cheerful' and 'undefeated'. This makes you
feel (8) ............ enormous sympathy for the old man. You
want him to bring home another fish (9) ............ soon, before
he becomes (10) ............ old to go out to sea.

The main reason why the book is (11) ............ popular is
that it tells a (12) ............ simple story that is timeless
(13) ............ to appeal to people of all ages and backgrounds.
It has (14) ............ an unusual style, (15) ............ , which
contributes to its success.

**G → Student's Book page 173**

# Listening

**5** 🔊 **10** You will hear a radio interview with a woman who has done a survey on attitudes to ebooks. For questions 1–7, choose the best answer (A, B or C).

**1** The idea of doing a survey on ebooks came from
A a market research company.
B a university tutor.
C Anna herself.

**2** What did Anna find surprising about the survey results?
A that some older people won't even try reading ebooks
B that her generation aren't entirely positive about ebooks
C that middle-aged people complain about the cost of ebooks

**3** Anna believes that the main benefit people attach to ebooks is
A the flexibility of being able to search through them.
B their availability to those living in remote locations.
C the capacity of the hardware to store so many ebooks.

**4** What does Anna believe will happen in book publishing?
A Ebooks will eventually replace hardback publications.
B Paperback sales will be the most affected by ebooks.
C Publishers will take over the selling of downloads.

**5** Anna says that the only disadvantage of ebooks to consumers is
A the fact that there may be a hidden extra cost involved.
B the issue of having to pay for additional unwanted features.
C the new threat to health through lack of physical movement.

**6** What is Anna's view on the changing position of authors in relation to ebooks?
A Authors will earn less money as a result of illegal copying.
B Ebooks will encourage authors who are unpublished to succeed.
C Few authors will require the services of an agent in the future.

**7** What is Anna's next career move?
A to set up her own company
B to follow up her ebooks research
C to team up with an interested firm

# An apple a day ...

## Reading

1   You are going to read a newspaper article about how dancing can be good for your health. For questions 1–6, choose the answer (A, B, C or D) which you think fits best according to the text.

**Flo Marsden, aged 71, is learning how to belly dance thanks to a local dance scheme in the UK. Janet Booth reports.**

Dance is increasingly being introduced to anyone who is interested for both health and recreational reasons. The National Lottery is funding courses and training, as are local authorities and regional arts associations. In addition, family doctors are prescribing dance to patients, and young footballers are learning about rhythm and balance through hip-hop lessons. There is barely a hall in the country that does not shudder with the sound of stamping feet every week.

The Yorkshire Dance Centre runs Flo's classes. Simon Dove, the dance centre's organiser and promoter, says that attendance has doubled in the last three years. He attributes this to more choice and easier access. And what a choice there is! There are 35 different lessons every week – everything from Arabic dancing to Egyptian, American tap, Asian and South African Township dance. 'Aerobics and fitness regimes can be an introspective and solitary way of keeping fit,' Simon explains. 'People like coming here because it helps you stay fit and engages your mind, enabling you to interact with others.'

Steve Johnson, 28, is one of the company's teachers. He goes into schools and introduces kids to jazz, street dance and hip-hop. He thinks that for the less academic, it gives them something to focus on. 'Several school teachers have reported back to me that normally difficult and disruptive children have become more manageable because of the lessons. I think it is because they have found something at school that they excel at, making them more confident. The lessons also make them more aware of their bodies and how they work.'

For Flo, who already keeps fit by doing aerobics, her weekly dance lessons play a more social role in her life. 'It's the togetherness of dancing that is the best. A keep fit class doesn't get you so involved with others. When I go out shopping I see people from the lessons and say hello. It makes you feel you are part of a community.'   *34*

Dance is one of the five activities the Health Education Authority is promoting in its current Active for Life campaign, and this summer saw one of the first health and dance conferences in the UK. John Dunbar, one of the speakers, says that on a fitness level, dance can be just as effective as going on a running programme: 'There were tests done in the US where two previously sedentary 30-year-olds were put on fitness programmes, one using dance, the other running, and the results were the same. People are far more likely to keep up dancing rather than a running programme, so in that way it can be more suitable.'

So, if you're lucky enough to have dance classes near where you live, my advice to you would be to have a go!

1   The dance classes are being paid for by
   A   the participants themselves.
   B   a variety of public bodies.
   C   family health centres.
   D   local sports centres.

2   What does Simon say about the dance classes in the second paragraph?
   A   Some are more popular than others.
   B   They are the quickest way to make friends.
   C   They are a very sociable way to exercise.
   D   There is no limit to the number you can take.

3   Steve Johnson believes that dance
   A   is suitable for the less active type of child.
   B   has grown in popularity in less academic schools.
   C   can be taught by ordinary school teachers.
   D   helps children who have low self-esteem.

4   Flo enjoys going to dance classes because
   A   they make her feel more relaxed than other classes.
   B   they provide her with a sense of belonging.
   C   they allow her to meet people from outside the area.
   D   they have enabled her to get over her shyness.

5   What does 'It' refer to in line 34?
   A   dancing
   B   a community
   C   keeping fit
   D   the social role

6   According to John Dunbar, dancing
   A   is much better for you than running.
   B   needs to be done regularly to be effective.
   C   has most effect on the health of older people.
   D   motivates people more than running.

# Vocabulary

**2** Make the change indicated to the words below and then read through the text in 1 to check you are correct.

**For example:**
region (adjective) = *regional*

**a** attend (noun) = ...........................................
**b** choose (noun) = ...........................................
**c** fit (noun) = ...........................................
**d** disrupt (adjective) = ...........................................
**e** manage (adjective) = ...........................................
**f** confidence (adjective) = ...........................................
**g** week (adjective) = ...........................................
**h** society (adjective) = ...........................................
**i** effect (adjective) = ...........................................
**j** suit (adjective) = ...........................................

**3** Find ten more words to do with health in this wordsearch. Some words are parts of the body and others are connected with doctors and hospitals. Words can be horizontal, vertical or diagonal. They may run forwards or backwards.

| B | A | N | D | A | G | E | B | H | L |
|---|---|---|---|---|---|---|---|---|---|
| G | N | D | H | W | A | L | L | C | Q |
| U | K | I | G | I | T | B | K | A | S |
| F | L | U | U | A | B | O | R | M | T |
| Y | E | R | O | Y | N | W | T | O | K |
| M | H | R | C | U | E | N | D | T | N |
| S | H | A | O | L | X | I | F | S | E |
| T | E | H | E | A | D | A | C | H | E |
| Q | R | Y | M | L | D | P | V | N | O |
| I | N | J | E | C | T | I | O | N | P |

# Grammar

**4** Complete the second sentence so that it has a similar meaning to the first sentence, using the word given. Do not change the word given. You must use between two and five words, including the word given.

**1** You really should try to stop smoking.
**HIGH**
It's ................................................................... smoking.

**2** What do you think I should do?
**ADVISE**
What ................................................................... do?

**3** He advised me to do some weight training.
**WERE**
'If ........................................... do some weight training,' he said.

**4** 'Why don't we go for a walk next weekend?' Anne said.
**SUGGESTED**
Anne ........................................................ for a walk the following weekend.

**5** Your teeth need checking regularly.
**HAVE**
You ought ........................................................... regularly.

**6** I would strongly advise you to get your blood pressure checked.
**TIME**
It's ........................................... blood pressure checked.

**7** It's not a good idea to sit in the sun for too long.
**BETTER**
You ........................................... in the sun for too long.

**G → Student's Book page 174**

# Writing

**5** In your English class you have been talking about health and fitness. Now your English teacher has asked you to write an essay.

Write an essay using all the notes and give reasons for your point of view.

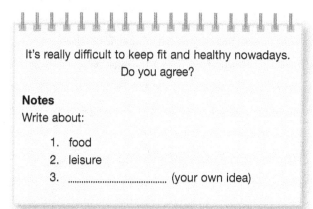

It's really difficult to keep fit and healthy nowadays. Do you agree?

**Notes**
Write about:

1. food
2. leisure
3. ........................................... (your own idea)

Write your essay in 140–190 words.

# No place to hide

## Listening

1  **1.11** You will hear a student called Dan talking about the famous detective Sherlock Holmes, who was created by the writer Sir Arthur Conan Doyle. For questions 1–10, complete the sentences with a word or short phrase.

Dan says Conan Doyle studied (1) ..................................... at the University of Edinburgh.

Conan Doyle based Sherlock Holmes on a (2) ..................................... he had met when he was a student.

Conan Doyle was particularly impressed by wax models of well-known (3) ..................................... which he saw on a visit to London.

Conan Doyle's first story about Sherlock Holmes was published in a (4) ..................................... in 1887.

Dan says that, in the stories, Sherlock Holmes seems to know a lot about the subject of (5) ..................................... .

Sherlock Holmes used forensic medicine, especially things like (6) ..................................... to find criminals.

Dan is surprised that Sherlock Holmes had a (7) ..................................... which he used to look for evidence.

Dan says that some fans of Sherlock Holmes find it strange that they no longer find (8) ..................................... in London.

Later in his life, Conan Doyle wanted to concentrate on writing (9) ..................................... fiction.

Dan says that the Sherlock Holmes Museum is interesting but that the (10) ..................................... is wrong for the period.

## Vocabulary

### Word formation

2  For questions 1–8, read the text below and use the word given in capitals to form a word that fits in the gap. There is an example at the beginning (0).

## White-collar crime

White-collar crime is defined as (0) **illegal** (LEGAL) acts committed by middle- or upper-class people while at work. The term gained (1) ..................................... (POPULAR) in 1940 when it was first used by the American criminologist Edwin H. Sutherland. Sutherland argued that there were important sociological (2) ..................................... (DIFFERENT) between conventional crimes such as (3) ..................................... (BURGLAR) and murder, and white-collar crimes such as fraud and income tax evasion. In general, the latter are committed by persons of (4) ..................................... (RELATIVE) high social status and are treated more leniently than more (5) ..................................... (CONVENTION) crimes. White-collar crime is an (6) ..................................... (INCREASE) problem. The authorities now dealing with such crimes more severely because of a growing feeling that an effort must be made to establish (7) ..................................... (EQUAL) before the law for all citizens – (8) ..................................... (REGARD) of money, power or social status.

# Grammar

**3** For questions 1–8, read the text below and think of the word which best fits each gap. Use only one word in each gap. There is an example at the beginning (0).

## A bad experience

Thank you **(0)** FOR the photos you sent me of our holiday together. It was great to remember **(1)** .......................... a good time we had, especially as I've not had a very happy time **(2)** ......................... I got back. **(3)** ......................... you know, I'm a member of the city choir and we meet every Wednesday to practise. Well, two weeks ago I went to the rehearsal as usual. However, on the way to the bus stop a young woman stopped me and asked me for directions to a local park. I thought it was rather strange as it was already dark and the park **(4)** ......................... definitely be closed. Anyway, as I was telling her she pushed me over and ran off with my handbag. I was **(5)** ......................... shocked I didn't know what to do. A few minutes later, although it felt **(6)** ......................... a few hours, someone came along the street and saw me **(7)** ......................... the ground. They were very helpful and took me to the local police station. I told the police what had happened but they think there's very **(8)** ......................... chance of my getting my bag back, unfortunately.

## Gerunds or infinitives 2

**4** Correct the following sentences where necessary.

**a** He suggested to buy a detective novel.
**b** I look forward to hear the results of the case.
**c** I enjoy watching American cop programmes.
**d** The burglar alarm needs look at.
**e** Let me giving you a description of the mugger.
**f** The prisoners were made to sew mail bags.
**g** I can't afford taking a taxi all the time just to avoid the underground.
**h** The tourist was accustomed to drive his car faster in his country.
**i** You are not allowed dropping litter on the street.
**j** I'd like reporting a burglary.
**k** She's too young to drive a car.

**G** → Student's Book page 174

# Writing

Thank you so much for inviting me

perhaps we will meet again soon

looking forward to your talk on 5th November

marvellous that you can tell

My family and I would love to come

So much from a person's handwriting

we spent the day at their house

sorry I haven't written for so long

**5** Read through this article on graphology, and correct it. There are 12 spelling errors.

Graphology is the study and analysis of handwriting in order to asess the writer's personality. In crime detection, graphology is used to determine the authenticity of a signature or docuement, such as a will or a manuscript, witout concern for the writer's personality. Graphologists need at least a full-page ink specimen, writen spontaneously under normal phisical conditions, by a person able to write with ease. Before the analysis, the graphologist must know the writer's age, sex and nationality, none of wich is revealed by the writing itself. Handwriting consits of measureable elements, such as slant and size, and of descriptive elements, such as letter form and tendencies to the right and left. However, allthough the results of handwriting analysis sometimes correspond impresively with experimental evidence, graphology has still not been fully acepted as a legitimate branch of phsychology.

# Urban decay, suburban hell

## Reading

1  Read this article quickly, ignoring the missing sentences.
   Decide which of the descriptions below best summarises its content.

   a  A guide to amenities in the modern city
   b  The changing patterns in city lifestyles
   c  Opening hours for shopping in some cities

# Time and the city

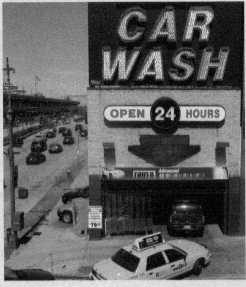

In modern cities, it is now time as much as space that separates urban functions, as people's lives are lived not only to different timetables, but also at wildly different rates. The mass timetable of the industrial city, with its factory sirens for the men at dawn and dusk, 9–5 office hours for the women and silent Sundays, has gone. In its place is flexi-time, part-time working, Sunday shopping and the 24-hour city.

European cities are responding to these changes perhaps faster than British cities. In at least half a dozen cities in Italy, for example, you will find the *Uffici Tempi* – the Offices of Time. What they do is try to reorganise time more flexibly in the city, in order to meet new needs. [1       ] Usually located in the Mayor's office, the *Uffici Tempi* bring together transport providers, shop-owners, employers, trade unions, the police and other services to see how their efforts might be better harmonised. The main aim in all this is to increase the efficiency and productivity of the city. This can mean staggering the starting times in schools, offices and factories to avoid rush hours, or having shops opening later in the day but closing later too. [2       ]

In a number of German cities, people have been debating whether the timetable of the future city should be 6 × 6 or 4 × 9 – working hours, that is. [3       ] This would give employees more time in the afternoons to be with children or to get the shopping.

In Britain, public leisure provision was one of the earliest sectors to respond to the need to adapt to changing time patterns. [4       ] The Oasis leisure centre in Swindon, from which the rock band took its name, has operated a 20-hour day, seven days a week, for at least a decade.

[5       ] After all, who likes working evenings or Sundays? Nevertheless, many city centres are now open for shopping seven days a week, and a number of them now promote themselves as '24-hour cities', where those with money can drink, eat, dance and even shop the whole night.

Time is flexible, but buildings aren't. [6       ] Adaptability has become the key skill. We are slowly abandoning the terminology of dormitory suburbs and industrial districts, in favour of mixed-use areas, out-of-town retailing and working from home. There is no doubt that planning theory is being challenged by the changing nature of time in the modern city.

**2** Now choose from the sentences A–G the one which fits each gap (1–6). There is one extra sentence which you do not need.

**A** One further benefit is that there can be more police about in the evening, patrolling the streets when people most need them.

**B** Apparently male workers favour a four-day week, while women workers, on the other hand, favour six shorter working days.

**C** The need for public services to adapt to our changing lifestyles has been quite difficult for some of the staff involved.

**D** This is particularly relevant for Italian women, an increasing number of whom have to balance two timetables: work and home.

**E** These time shifts aren't always beneficial and can lead to conflict between households.

**F** It is interesting how often in modern consumer societies it is this industry which seems to anticipate or forecast social change.

**G** The mismatch between the fabric of the city and its uses, over time, is a serious architectural and planning problem.

**3** Find words in the article to complete this table.

| Verb | Noun |
|---|---|
| adapt | |
| | harmony |
| | location |
| produce | |
| | promotion |
| provide | |
| | response |

# Grammar

## Mixed conditionals

**4** Match the two halves of these sentences and then say which ones are mixed conditionals.

1 If Carmen wasn't so rude,
2 If I had more space in this flat,
3 If you hadn't grabbed that waiter,
4 If we had booked the flight earlier,
5 If the council had gone ahead,
6 If they lived closer to us,

a we would still be waiting to order.
b I would have visited them.
c I would buy a grand piano.
d several people would be out of a job.
e I would have gone to her party.
f we would have got a good reduction.

**G** → Student's Book page 175

# Vocabulary

## Word formation

**5** For questions 1–8, read the text below. Use the word given in capitals at the end of some of the lines to form a word that fits in the gap in the same line. There is an example at the beginning (0).

### KEEPING CITY CENTRES ALIVE

City centres are dynamic and change is
**(0)** __UNAVOIDABLE__. This is **AVOID**
particularly true nowadays, when new out-
of-town complexes are threatening the
**(1)** .............................. of old, established **EXIST**
shops. A central **(2)** .............................. is **LOCATE**
no longer as attractive to the public, due to
traffic problems and parking restrictions.

The most **(3)** .............................. city centres **SUCCESS**
are the ones that evolve to meet the new
**(4)** .............................. of their users. **REQUIRE**
A local council may need to seek private
**(5)** .............................. in order to pay for the **FUND**
complete **(6)** .............................. of the city **GENERATE**
centre. Government help is, at the moment,
**(7)** .............................. to be available, **LIKE**
although this policy may well be
**(8)** .............................. in the future. **CONSIDER**

# A world of music

## Vocabulary

1 For questions 1–8, read the text below and decide which answer (A, B, C or D) best fits each gap. There is an example at the beginning (0).

**Example:**

0   **A** crammed          **B** filled          **C** pressed          **D** placed

**Answer: A**

# The sonic tool that has shaped pop music

Imagine having a full orchestra (**0**) ............. into your house. For a start, with so many people, it would get very stuffy indeed. The patience of the (**1**) ............. would soon wear thin. Also, you would need earplugs for the percussion, and the brass section would probably drink everything in your fridge. An acceptable alternative is (**2**) ............. by the sampler, a piece of equipment that records, edits and mixes a wide variety of sounds electronically – the musical equivalent of a word processor.

The sampler can alter the length of sounds – for example, it can (**3**) ............. down the human voice to create something very unusual. Another feature is that the recorded sound can be (**4**) ............. back at any pitch – the woof of a small dog can be (**5**) ............. into a Bark prelude and fugue!

1980s 'synth-pop' (**6**) ............. extensive use of the sampler. It was customary to include orchestral 'stabs': a single, short (**7**) ............. from an entire symphony orchestra inside a tin box. Then hip-hop music (**8**) ............. and people started using the sampler for rhythm, stealing four bars of drumming off an old record to provide the backbeat for a whole song. It could be said that the sampler is every instrument and none, but it certainly gives endless possibilities to musicians everywhere.

| | | | |
|---|---|---|---|
| **1 A** controller | **B** governor | **C** driver | **D** conductor |
| **2 A** handled | **B** offered | **C** shown | **D** suggested |
| **3 A** cut | **B** hold | **C** slow | **D** keep |
| **4 A** carried | **B** gone | **C** played | **D** run |
| **5 A** got | **B** turned | **C** exchanged | **D** set |
| **6 A** did | **B** put | **C** drew | **D** made |
| **7 A** note | **B** key | **C** sign | **D** remark |
| **8 A** caused | **B** became | **C** happened | **D** produced |

**2** Find the odd word out in each of the sets a–h, giving reasons for your answers.

**a** cello   harp   performance   oboe
**b** violinist   pianist   flautist   conductor
**c** gig   rehearsal   concert   show
**d** piece   key   sonata   symphony
**e** improvise   compose   perform   play
**f** duo   soloist   quartet   orchestra
**g** venue   hall   room   stage
**h** wind   strings   cello   percussion

# Writing

**3** Read the following article about live concerts. Then put clauses A–G into the correct gaps (1–6) in the article. There is one extra clause, which you do not need to use.

Seeing live music

There's something very special about going to a live concert. Although CDs are wonderful, allowing you to listen to your favourite band in the comfort of your own home, they cannot create the true atmosphere of a live performance. **(1)** ............ or booked them online months before, you get the same feeling of excitement when you finally make it into the concert venue. **(2)** ............ , you eventually see the road crew leave the stage. **(3)** ............ , with everyone around you yelling and screaming, as the musicians come on stage? **(4)** ............ , you soon get carried away by the rhythm and power of the music. **(5)** ............ , the audience around you rocks and sways to the beat of each song. **(6)** ............ , you stomp your feet and shout for more, and are rewarded at last by the sight of the band running back on stage for that final encore. Give me live music every time!

> **A** How can you keep still after that
> **B** Even if it is not your favourite band
> **C** Whether you have queued up for tickets
> **D** And when it seems to be over
> **E** Standing with thousands of other fans
> **F** Like powerful waves out at sea
> **G** This is doubly true then

# Listening

**4** 🔘 **1.12** You will hear people talking in six different situations. For questions 1–6, choose the best answer (A, B or C).

**1** You hear a professional musician talking about his work. What type of music does he play?
**A** rock
**B** jazz
**C** classical

**2** You hear a man and a woman talking about a band. What does the woman say about their latest album?
**A** She recognises a lot of the tunes.
**B** She finds the words of the songs interesting.
**C** She thinks the album is better than their last one.

**3** You hear a boy and a girl talking about their guitar lessons. What is the boy's problem?
**A** He feels he isn't improving enough.
**B** He believes the lessons aren't long enough.
**C** He wonders whether he is doing enough practice.

**4** You hear part of a radio interview with a female singer. Where do most of her current earnings come from?
**A** her solo albums
**B** her advertising work
**C** her concert performances

**5** You hear a composer talking about his latest work. The biggest influence on this piece of music was
**A** the sounds of city streets.
**B** the ideas of his students.
**C** the countryside of his youth.

**6** You hear a man and a woman talking about an open-mic night. Who was the best performer at this week's event?
**A** a violinist
**B** a bass guitarist
**C** a keyboard player

# 23 Unexpected events

## Vocabulary

**1** Find nine more words to do with weather in this wordsearch. Words can be horizontal or vertical.

| Y | L | I | G | H | T | N | I | N | G |
|---|---|---|---|---|---|---|---|---|---|
| F | Z | T | V | U | T | N | K | R | O |
| L | H | H | O | S | S | N | O | W | S |
| O | X | U | S | T | O | R | M | A | F |
| O | Z | N | J | Q | K | O | U | I | L |
| D | I | D | S | H | O | W | E | R | A |
| K | E | E | Q | I | R | E | D | N | S |
| F | O | R | E | C | A | S | T | A | H |
| O | I | R | A | I | N | D | R | O | P |
| H | U | R | R | I | C | A | N | E | E |

**2** Now complete these sentences with the words you have found. Use plural forms if necessary.

a Many ..................... are given men and women's names.

b The ..................... came down so heavily last night that my car was completely buried.

c Liz saw a ..................... of ..................... in the sky above the mountain.

d On the radio it said that a ..................... is likely so I wouldn't go out if I were you.

e I was woken up by the sound of small ..................... hitting my window.

f Take an umbrella – ..................... are expected later.

g Their brother always hides under the bed when he hears the sound of ..................... .

h Can we always rely on the weather ..................... ?

i After the ..................... the water level didn't go down for a few weeks.

## Reading

**3** Before you read the text on page 49, think about the following questions and decide whether they are true or false.

a There is a fair chance you will be struck by lightning.

b Many forest fires are started by lightning.

c You must keep away from trees if there is a chance of lightning striking.

d If you are caught in a storm, you should crouch down as low as possible on the ground.

**4** Now skim the text quickly to see if you can find the answers to the questions above.

**5** For questions 1–10, choose from the sections (A–F). The sections may be chosen more than once.

**Which section**

talks about a gadget? `1` [ ]

mentions a person who only seemed unharmed on the outside? `2` [ ]

mentions victims being in an enclosed space? `3` [ ]

mentions a myth? `4` [ ]

describes how someone felt when they were struck? `5` [ ]

mentions possible warning signs of a lightning strike? `6` [ ]

blames lightning for certain natural disasters? `7` [ ]

recommends the best position to get into? `8` [ ]

mentions keeping souvenirs of being hit? `9` [ ]

mentions someone who made a discovery about lightning? `10` [ ]

# Lightning strikes!

**A** Three years ago a bolt of lightning all but destroyed Lyn Miller's house in Aberdeen – with her two children inside. 'There was a huge rainstorm,' she says, recalling the terrifying experience. 'My brother and I were outside desperately working to stop floodwater from coming in the house. Suddenly I was thrown to the ground by an enormous bang. When I picked myself up, the roof and the entire upper storey of the house had been demolished. The door was blocked by rubble, but we forced our way in and found the children, thankfully unharmed. Later I was told that being struck by lightning is a chance in a million.' In fact, it's calculated at one chance in 600,000. Even so, Dr Mark Keys of AER Technology, an organisation that monitors the effects of lightning, thinks you should be sensible. 'I wouldn't go out in a storm – but then I'm quite a careful person.' He advises anyone who is unlucky enough to be caught in a storm to get down on the ground and curl up into a ball, making yourself as small as possible.

**B** Lightning is one of nature's most awesome displays of sheer power. No wonder the ancient Greeks thought it was Zeus, father of the gods, throwing thunderbolts around in anger. 250 years ago, Benjamin Franklin, the American scientist and statesman, proved that lightning is a form of electricity, but scientists still lack a complete understanding of how it works.

**C** Occasionally there are indications that lightning may strike. Positive electrical charges streaming upwards from trees or church spires may glow and make a buzzing noise, and people's hair can stand on end. And if you fear lightning, you'll be glad to know that a company in the USA has manufactured a hand-held lightning detector which can detect it up to 70 km away, sound a warning tone and monitor the storm's approach.

**D** Lizzie Anne Bright was on a camping trip when lightning struck a tree and then travelled to where she was sitting. 'The feeling I got is hard to explain. I felt as if I was rising above the ground. I couldn't move and my shoulder really hurt and had burns. I was in hospital for five days. I still keep the clothes I was wearing that day. My jacket has a large black hole in it and my trousers and socks just melted.'

**E** Harold Deal, a retired electrician from South Carolina, USA, was struck by lightning 26 years ago. He was apparently unhurt, but it later emerged that the strike had damaged the part of the brain which controls the sensation of temperature. Since then the freezing South Carolina winters haven't bothered Harold, since he is completely unable to feel the cold.

**F** Animals are victims of lightning too. Hundreds of cows and sheep are killed every year, largely because they go under trees. In East Anglia in 1918, 504 sheep were killed instantaneously by the same bolt of lightning that hit the ground and travelled through the entire flock. Lightning is also responsible for starting more than 10,000 forest fires each year world-wide.

**6** Find words in the text which are the opposite of these words. They are all in the order you read them.

a outside .............................................

b forgetting .............................................

c tiny .............................................

d lower .............................................

e irresponsible .............................................

f fortunate .............................................

g partial .............................................

h frequently .............................................

i negative .............................................

j boiling .............................................

# Grammar

## I wish / If only

**7** Correct the following sentences, if necessary.

a I hope I would see you soon.

b I wish I would go to visit you.

c Mary said she wished she had been able to come to your party last weekend.

d I hope your family are well.

e If only you manage to give up smoking, just think of the money you'd save.

f I hope the weather would stay nice for you.

g I wish my sister would come and see me sometime.

h I wish I haven't seen that film about earthquakes – I can't sleep at night now.

i I wish to inform you of my move to a new job.

j Dave wishes he knows more about earthquakes.

**G → Student's Book page 175**

# Anything for a laugh

## Vocabulary

### Word formation

1 For questions 1–8, read the text below. Use the word in capitals at the end of some of the lines to form a word that fits in the gap in the same line. There is an example at the beginning (0).

Sitting in a bath of baked beans to raise money.

# RED N⬤SE DAY

| | |
|---|---|
| Red Nose Day is one of Britain's most **(0)** __SUCCESSFUL__ events, raising money for good causes. It is organised by the charity Comic Relief and takes place in March. Many well-known **(1)** ........................... take part, as well as actors, musicians, TV personalities and other celebrities. One year, the singer Jessie J shaved off all her hair and raised a **(2)** ........................... sum of money by doing that. | **SUCCEED** **COMEDY** **SUBSTANCE** |
| In addition to a great evening's **(3)** ........................... on TV on the day itself, there are many programmes and live events in the weeks leading up to Red Nose Day. At schools and colleges, students do silly things for cash, like sitting in a bath full of cold baked beans! Many workplaces organise **(4)** ........................... stunts and donate money. Shops and supermarkets sell the famous red noses and other **(5)** ........................... such as red hair dye and badges. | **ENTERTAIN** **SAME** **PRODUCE** |
| Through short documentary films, TV **(6)** ........................... learn how the money raised in previous years has helped Comic Relief to make a real **(7)** ........................... to people in need, both in Britain and in Africa. Some of the stories shown are shocking, but the message is always a positive one and there are many happy **(8)** ........................... . Comic Relief has achieved a great deal by making people laugh. | **VIEW** **DIFFERENT** **END** |

2 Fill in the missing words in these jokes to do with crime.

a Don't you know that crime doesn't ........................... ?
   – I know, but the hours are good.

b Order, order in the ...........................!
   – Thank you, Judge. I'll have a ham and cheese on rye bread.

c He went to jail for something he didn't do – he didn't ........................... his taxes!

d Are you guilty or ........................... guilty?
   – That seems a rather personal question, Judge!

# Listening

3  **1 13** You will hear an interview with a comedian called Kate Gordon. For questions 1–7, choose the best answer (A, B or C).

1  Kate's recent award is for
   A  her TV writing.
   B  her live comedy act.
   C  her part in a radio show.

2  As a female comedian, Kate
   A  believes that it is important to find the right venue.
   B  finds it hard to combine her work with her family.
   C  accepts that it is still an unequal profession.

3  What does Kate say about writing new material?
   A  It needs to be revised following its first performance.
   B  It can be good to base jokes around a particular audience.
   C  It shouldn't take her as much time to develop as it does.

4  How does Kate find her best ideas for jokes?
   A  by searching on the internet
   B  by asking her friends things
   C  by watching people carefully

5  What is Kate's attitude to a possible career in film?
   A  She would prefer to work with an experienced director.
   B  She has concerns about the quality of many film scripts.
   C  She feels unsure whether such a large team would be fun.

6  Kate gets most nervous when performing
   A  in a small club.
   B  at her local theatre.
   C  in the open air.

7  What advice would Kate give about starting in comedy?
   A  watch a lot of comedy shows
   B  practise your material at home
   C  get in front of an audience early on

# Grammar

4  Complete the second sentence so that it has a similar meaning to the first sentence, using the word given. Do not change the word given. You must use between two and five words, including the word given.

1  How can you stand these tasteless jokes?
   **PUT**
   How can you ................................................ these tasteless jokes?

2  I prefer to see live comedy instead of watching TV recordings of it.
   **THAN**
   I would ................................................ watch TV recordings of it.

3  The flight attendant told us to shut down our computers in preparation for landing.
   **OFF**
   We were told by the flight attendant to ................................................ the plane was preparing to land.

4  The customs officer demanded to know what was in his suitcase.
   **INSISTED**
   The customs officer ................................................ of his suitcase.

5  His boss told him he was fired and ordered him to leave immediately.
   **GOT**
   His boss told him he ................................................ and said he should leave immediately.

6  I'd prefer to get going now, before it gets dark.
   **RATHER**
   I ................................................ until it gets dark, so I'll get going now.

# Answers and recording scripts

## Unit 1

### Vocabulary

#### Spellcheck

1 hairstyle; outrageous; jewellery (or 'jewelry' in US English);
bracelets; earrings; expensive; exciting; suits;
fashion-conscious; different

2 a imagine
   b beautiful
   c brilliant
   d beginning
   e writer
   f apologise
   g disappointed
   h Happiness

#### Phrasal verbs

3 a keep up with
   b pulled on
   c get away with; smarten … up
   d dressed up; stood out
   e put together

### Reading

4 They date from 1886.

5 a False – there is one other pair, according to the text
   b False – he paid even more for them
   c True – the company historian
   d False – they have a leather patch
   e True
   f True

6 oldest; the most expensive; the highest; the most important

7 a excessive    b ordinary    c appropriately
   d delighted    e frayed    f remarkably

### Grammar

#### Comparison

8 b Flat shoes are more comfortable than high-heeled ones.
   c Jeans are more casual than trousers.
   d Supermodels are thinner than other people.
   e Lily Cole is younger than Kate Moss.
   f New York is bigger than San Francisco.
   g Jogging is less dangerous than bungee-jumping.
   h Clubbing is more/less tiring than studying.

9 a not as cheap as
   b not as difficult as
   c not as fast as

## Unit 2

### Listening

1  1 D   2 G   3 H   4 E   5 B

---

**Recording script** 1 02

*You will hear five short extracts in which people are talking about computer games. For questions 1–5, choose from the list (A–H) the job of each person. Use the letters only once. There are three extra letters which you do not need to use.*

*You now have 30 seconds to look at the questions.*

*Speaker 1*

The trend in society is to label computer games as mindless and anti-social, but I don't share that view. Many of the problem teenagers that we care for at the centre need to develop relationships and improve their social skills. Introducing computer games in an early session often allows me to get through to these kids and to win their confidence. I also find that playing these games often makes them feel better about themselves, and that is so important.

*Speaker 2*

Some games are very violent and have extremely graphic content – lots of blood and gunfire. I worry about what that might be doing to a young person who already has emotional issues of some kind. I know the evidence isn't conclusive, but some of the problem cases I have to deal with in my classroom really make me think that there could be a link between violent games and aggressive behaviour.

*Speaker 3*

I never played computer games much myself when I was young. The kids I look after are only eight and ten, and I feel it's not good for them to be exposed to so much violence. But their mum and dad let them play with this stuff at the weekends, so I'm in a rather tricky position. It's always easier when the weather's good and we can get out to the park to play football, but on a rainy afternoon, I find it hard to say no sometimes.

*Speaker 4*

My job's great! I've always been into Manga and cartoons, so working on the visual side of all these fantastic new games we're developing is pure fun! We often work late to finish a project and it can take ages getting a particular image right, but it's great when you finally succeed. I'd like to move into animation work in the future and they may be willing to send me on a training course for that some day.

## Reading

2 board games

3 a business  b appreciate  c interrupting
  d working out problems  e chance  f limit
  g keen  h plonk

## Grammar

### Review of present tenses

4 *Suggested verbs*
  a5 says; are rising
  b1 believe; offer
  c3 are spending; means
  d4 are stopping; think
  e2 seem; involve

5 1 know  2 like  3 keeps  4 realises/knows
  5 forgets/hates  6 hate  7 likes
  8 sounds  9 understands  10 wish

## Vocabulary

6 Vertical word: internet
  1 graphics  2 clone  3 adventure
  4 opponent  5 version  6 weapons
  7 solve  8 effects

7 a anti-social  b messy  c demanding
  d aggressive  e sophisticated

## Unit 3

## Vocabulary

### Travel quiz

1 a cruise  b tourists  c ferry
  d yacht  e hotels  f harbour
  g cabin  h travel agent  i flight

### Phrasal verbs

2 1 g  2 f  3 b  4 e
  5 h  6 a  7 c  8 d

3 a feel like  b depart for  c put up with
  d ring up  e recovering from  f continue

4 a Formal, written  f Formal, spoken
  b Informal, written  g Formal, written
  c Formal, written  h Informal/semi-formal, written
  d Formal, spoken  i Informal, spoken
  e Informal, spoken  j Informal, spoken

## Grammar

### Obligation, necessity and permission

5 a have to / must  e let
  b have to / must  f had to
  c don't have to  g needn't
  d need  h isn't permitted

### Prepositions of location

6 1 off  2 in  3 on  4 on  5 across/over
  6 round/around  7 on  8 in  9 to  10 to

## Unit 4

## Reading

1 a Africa  b San Diego
  c the silver-maned drill monkey  d four  e eight

### Guessing unknown words

3 a to restart / start again with a new population of animals
  b beginning
  c no longer on Earth
  d a discovery / significant development
  e to make/grow
  f stored/kept
  g metal containers
  h edge
  i a small pool of water
  j seeing

## Listening

4 1 insects  2 biology  3 pandas  4 rain/wet (weather)
  5 food  6 talks  7 finger  8 radio  9 teachers
  10 China

---

**Recording script**  **1** 03

*You will hear a zoo keeper called Helena Tomkins, talking about her work. For questions 1–10, complete the sentences with a word or short phrase.*

*You now have 45 seconds to look at the questions.*

**Helena:** Hello. Thank you for inviting me here to talk to you today. I've wanted to work with animals ever since I was four or five years old. What really interested me was not looking after cats or dogs like other children, but lying in the long grass watching <u>insects</u>. That interest in nature stayed with me throughout my childhood and when fairly young, I decided to become a zoo keeper.

In order to achieve my aim I had to work hard to get into university. I did <u>biology</u>, though for my job you can do a variety of different degrees as long as they have some connection with animals – things like zoology obviously, and psychology and animal science are fine too.

When you're appointed as a zoo keeper, you generally work with just one species of animal. I worked with the sea lions for a couple of years but for the last few months I've been in charge of the <u>pandas</u>, which is particularly exciting as they're an endangered species and we have a special breeding programme in place.

There are some downsides to being a zoo keeper. We sometimes have to work quite long hours, sometimes all night, especially in the hospital when an animal's sick, but I don't really mind that as it's part of the job. What does get me, however, is the <u>rain</u>. It's quite hard to make yourself go outside when it's wet. Even the animals don't like it!

My typical day usually starts around seven o'clock. I guess the main task I have in the morning is getting the <u>food</u> ready. I don't clean out the enclosures. Someone else is responsible for that. Then, in the afternoon, I write up health reports or assist with any medical procedures. On Saturdays and Wednesdays I also do <u>talks</u>, but that's only in the summer when we have a lot of visitors. In the winter it's obviously much quieter and I can get more involved in research projects.

The animals I look after can be dangerous so you need to take care when you're around them. Early on in my career, a monkey bit my <u>finger</u> but I only needed a few stitches. Someone else I worked with had his arm bitten by a tiger, so I've been lucky! That sort of thing doesn't happen very often though, I'm pleased to say!

I don't have to carry a stick or anything to protect myself, but what you do have to have with you is a <u>radio</u> and if we get on that, someone'll come running immediately. It's always good to know that there are other people around to give you a hand if things get difficult with an animal.

The visitors are usually great, especially the children. The people who do irritate me though are sometimes the <u>teachers</u> who bring their class to the zoo. They often don't spend enough time talking to their pupils, explaining about each animal. I think they see it as a day out really. It's a pity as it's a missed opportunity I always think.

As to the future, you do get attached to the animals you're looking after, so it would be hard for me to leave them at the moment. However, there are a couple of things I might do in the future. I've been offered the chance to go to <u>China</u> next spring to see how my animals behave in the wild. There's also a possibility of going to the USA to work on a breeding project, but that's not going to happen for a few years yet.

I do hope what I've told you has given you some insight into what I do. I can definitely recommend being a zoo keeper!

## Grammar

*as* and *like*

5 **a** as (well) as   **b** like   **c** like   **d** as
  **e** as   **f** as   **g** like

## Compound adjectives

6 **a** duty-free   **b** cross-eyed   **c** long-distance
  **d** absent-minded   **e** hand-made   **f** first-class
  **g** second-class/second-hand   **h** self-catering/self-made
  **i** right-handed/right-hand/right-minded

7 **a** hand-made/second-hand   **b** long-distance
  **c** second-hand
  **d** cross-eyed/absent-minded/right-handed
  **e** duty-free   **f** first-class/second-class   **g** self-catering

## Unit 5
### Vocabulary

1  1 disaster      2 compensation   3 dreadful
   4 earlier       5 worse          6 unhelpful
   7 worried       8 opposite       9 surprised
   10 thought      11 meant         12 spend
   13 conditions   14 stiff         15 refund

### Grammar

Review of past tenses

2

| Infinitive | Past tense | Past participle |
|---|---|---|
| blow | blew | blown |
| find | found | found |
| grab | grabbed | grabbed |
| hold | held | held |
| keep | kept | kept |
| realise | realised | realised |
| shake | shook | shaken |
| sink | sank | sunk |
| try | tried | tried |
| wave | waved | waved |

3  1 saw        2 knew    3 had taken    4 tried
   5 happened   6 went    7 realised     8 had interfered

*Suggested endings*

**a** The cliff was getting nearer and nearer, so Harry threw himself out of the window and landed on the ground, unharmed. The car went over the cliff.

**b** He swerved into a field on his left and noticed the largest pile of hay he had ever seen. He thought quickly. He drove into the haystack and thankfully survived.

**c** Harry went to pieces and screamed and shouted as the car went over the cliff. It landed 200 metres below and burst into flames, with Harry inside.

### Reading

4  1 F   2 E   3 B   4 A   5 F   6 B   7 C   8 D
   9 F   10 D

## Unit 6
### Listening

1  1 A   2 C   3 B   4 B   5 C   6 C

## Recording script ① 04

*You will hear people talking in six different situations. For questions 1–6, choose the best answer (A, B or C).*

### Question 1
*You hear a man telling a woman about a new musical.*

**Man:** I've just been to see that new musical that everyone's talking about.

**Woman:** Oh really, and is the plot as good as people say? I think the writer has won awards for his earlier work.

**Man:** Yeah, and it's not bad at all, although there are one or two bits that didn't work, which I got rather irritated by. For me, what stood out was <u>the people playing the two leading roles</u>. They were excellent, which is more than can be said for the songs. I found them unimpressive for the most part, just one cliché after another.

**Woman:** Well, it sounds as if I should go and see it sometime, anyway.

[The recording is repeated.]

### Question 2
*You hear a woman talking about a hotel.*

**Woman:** This five-star hotel may not be affordable for most of us, but it's frequently chosen by the rich and famous, who love to be photographed there. The hotel has been redeveloped by one of the world's most talented designers, and every room shows evidence of his style and flair. I was taken to the library for tea where I spent ages looking at the huge collection of leather-bound books displayed floor to ceiling on the longest walls. But when I tried to take one down, I realised that <u>they were all fake</u>! A library with unreadable books seems a departure from good taste to me, and I would personally knock a star off for it!

[The recording is repeated.]

### Question 3
*You hear a girl and a boy talking about being famous.*

**Girl:** So what would you find hard about your life if you became a superstar one day, a big footballer maybe? I hope you'd still treat me the same way!

**Boy:** Of course I would, Jackie, friendships don't change. I dunno, are there any drawbacks? You could basically have whatever you wanted … a nice car, a big house … You'd have plenty of money coming in and everyone would make a big fuss of you, wouldn't they?

**Girl:** I suppose you're right, but you can have too much attention, you know. And what about the publicity? I'd hate that side of it. <u>Imagine going out to the shops and having photographers following you down the street. What a hassle!</u>

**Boy:** That'd be fun! I'm sure you'd get used to it, anyway. It's part of the lifestyle.

[The recording is repeated.]

### Question 4
*You hear an interview about swimwear.*

**Interviewer:** I'm with Liam O'Neill, and we're surrounded by his latest range of swimwear that's caused a real sensation here <u>at the *Clothes Show*</u>. Liam, why do you think you've done so well this year?

**Liam:** It's unbelievable, isn't it? … I dunno, it's kind of strange. The new stores have created a lot of interest throughout the country and I guess <u>people wanted to come and see for themselves</u>.

**Interviewer:** Liam, your <u>display</u> is most impressive – how did you move all that sand?

**Liam:** We had three lorries driving through the night to get here – it just wouldn't be right to launch swimwear without the beach!

[The recording is repeated.]

### Question 5
*You hear a woman talking on the phone.*

**Woman:** Hello, is that the news desk of the *Daily Times*? Yes, I'm ringing with some information … you see, I'm a close friend of Heather Woods … last week's jackpot winner, that's right. <u>I know she doesn't want any publicity but if the price is right, I'm willing to give you a story</u>. I mean it's ridiculous, all that money and she's sitting there miserably! I could visit your office tomorrow … or email you something if you prefer. … OK, that sounds interesting, my number's 0208 …

[The recording is repeated.]

### Question 6
*You overhear a man calling a hotel.*

**Man:** Good afternoon. It's Jack White again – I called you this morning and made a booking for three nights next week, a double room with bath? Well, I've checked with my wife and the room booking is fine so no changes there, but <u>I'd like to check something</u>. You told me the room rate would include breakfast but not dinner, yet <u>the advertisement on your website claims that IS included for all bookings made in March. So it must apply to us, surely?</u> … OK, I'll hold for the manager, thank you …

[The recording is repeated.]

## Grammar

### Conditionals with *if* and *unless*

2  **a** hadn't bought  **b** claims  **c** offered  **d** phones
   **e** grabbed  **f** hadn't been  **g** wasn't/weren't  **h** ended up

3  **a** Lottery winners **usually** find it difficult to sleep after they have heard the news.
   **b** I **rarely** have time to read long novels these days.
   **c** People are **always** telling me to stop working so hard.
   **d** Before the storm, I **never** worried about those trees near the house.
   **e** Now, if it's windy, I'm **often** worried that they'll fall on us.
   **f** What's happened to John? He's **normally** here by this time.

**4** 1 if you don't leave
  2 impossible to request
  3 (just) in case I
  4 never miss / never fail to watch
  5 hardly got/had any sleep
  6 able to keep up with
  7 enjoy being
  8 in danger due/owing

## Vocabulary

**5** a talent (not necessarily to do with being famous); nouns
  b give (not receiving); verbs
  c delight (positive feeling); nouns
  d irritated (different emotion); adjectives
  e keep away (not to do with solving problems); phrasal verbs
  f rarely (opposite meaning); adverbs

## Writing

**6** a I don't go to the theatre very often because there isn't one in my town.
  b (Please) could I use your phone (please)?
  c (Yesterday) I bought her a lovely blue silk dress (yesterday).
  d Alan never used to be keen on swimming.
  e Quite a few members of the audience were students.
  f I would eat Italian food when I lived in New York.
  g The crowd watched quietly as they pulled down the old cinema.
  h The man asked him if he could give him some money.
  i Not only does Alison like bananas/apples, she is also keen on apples/bananas.
  j I have never been so horrified in my life.

# Unit 7
## Reading

**1** 1 E  2 A  3 B  4 G  5 C  6 F

## Grammar

### Gerunds and infinitives 1

**2** a Jenny suggested **going** to the party in a taxi.
  b I look forward to **hearing** from you in the near future.
  c I don't mind **doing** it.
  d I'm interested **in learning** Spanish.
  e Correct
  f I'll help you with your homework when I finish **writing** my letter.
  g I am used to **doing** the washing-up.
  h Correct
  i Correct
  j I'm going to town **to** buy a new jumper.
  k I object to **paying** to park my car.
  l I can't afford to **lend** you any more money.
  m Correct

## Vocabulary

**3** a win  b nil  c referee  d court
  e clubs  f give  g laps

## Writing

**4** *Punctuated report*

Report on the regional college football competition held on 3rd May

Venue

This year the competition was held at Highworth College. This was an excellent choice of venue as there are six football pitches available, all in excellent condition.

The competition

All the teams in the competition were very experienced and played to a good level. This provided excellent entertainment for the spectators. The matches got off to a slow start, mainly because of the bad weather – it rained heavily throughout the morning but this cleared up after lunch. Then, there were a few incidents where the referee's decision was questioned, but generally the matches were all played in a positive way with good team spirit.

The result

The two finalists were Chedbury Manor College and Fulbrook High. The final score was 2–0 to Chedbury and it was a good win for them. Their striker was particularly impressive and could perhaps even be considered for a professional club if he wanted to take that route. All in all, a very good day's sport.

**5** *Suggested answer*

Hi Kim

It was great to hear from you and I'm really looking forward to you coming to my college. It's a great place and pretty well-known for sport. For swimming, it's necessary to go into the town as our college doesn't have a swimming pool. There's a really good one there and students get a discount. It's open every evening and at the weekend. I'm not sure about swimming competitions though.

We have a football team, which I'm on. I know you are a great goal-keeper so I'm sure there would be space for you! There are four pitches at the college and matches take place between different colleges every weekend during the season. When you arrive, go and see the coach, Mr Andrews – he used to play football professionally before he became the coach at our college.

We also have badminton and also hockey. You might also be interested to know that there's a gym which has some very up-to-date equipment. I go there in my lunch hour to work out. It's very popular so you have to put your name on the list the week before.

Can't wait for you to arrive!

# Unit 8
## Listening

**1** 1 H  2 F  3 C  4 E  5 A

**Recording script** 1 05

*You will hear five short extracts in which people are talking about the job they wanted to do when they were young. For questions 1–5, choose from the list (A to H) what each speaker says. Use the letters only once. There are three extra letters which you do not need to use.*

*You now have 30 seconds to look at the questions.*

*Speaker 1*

My dad used to own a restaurant and every weekend I had a job helping out in the kitchen. I guess he wanted me to be a chef or something like him. But I used to spend my time looking at the customers instead. I was fascinated by how they behaved – whether they would tip the waiters and why, things like that. I read lots of books on both animal and human behaviour too and ended up doing zoology at university and then becoming a university lecturer on that subject – a bit different from looking into people's minds, which is what I was keen on in my younger days.

*Speaker 2*

I guess everyone wants to do something really cool when they're young, don't they, like being a pop singer or flying to the moon on a space rocket. I never did really. I used to read lots of crime books when I was younger and try and copy the style. I think I saw myself as another Agatha Christie, producing loads of paperbacks. It's funny really as my sister joined a band and became quite famous. I ended up working in a zoo, looking after the elephants. I love it and can't imagine doing anything else now.

*Speaker 3*

I wasn't very good at school – only at music and drama. My teachers put me in all the stage productions we had. I would spend ages learning the words of the tunes till I was word perfect. I loved everything about it, from the costumes to standing on stage with the audience clapping – it was all I ever wanted to do. Anyway, things didn't turn out that way as I didn't get into drama school. Now I see real-life drama on the streets, investigating crime. I'm what they call a criminal psychologist. I still get to perform though – but usually in court, giving evidence.

*Speaker 4*

What was I like when I was young? Well, I loved helping my mum do the cooking and I was always reading science fiction. I never saw these as my future careers though. It was always animals for me, I guess. Nothing huge. More spiders and lizards. I could see myself spending my life taking care of them. Teaching the public about them too. My mum thought I was mad and spent her time trying to convince me to do enough schoolwork to go into science – maybe even be an astronaut!

*Speaker 5*

My brother wanted to be a famous detective. He even bought a magnifying glass and a notebook where he'd write down what the neighbours were doing. I think they must've thought he was a bit weird. I always did. He thought I was weird too, I guess. He'd make fun of me spending all my time in the kitchen following different recipes. He didn't mind eating the results, though. So, I reckon I must've done something right. And, I actually fulfilled my childhood ambition as I'm beginning to get quite well known now. He, on the other hand, is more normal and ended up as a teacher at our local college, teaching creative writing.

## Vocabulary

### Verb collocations

**2**  **a** does  **b** tastes  **c** spend  **d** had
 **e** spending  **f** keep  **g** broke

### Adverb–adjective collocations

**3**  highly praised, amusing
 deeply disappointed, ashamed
 perfectly happy, reasonable, serious

 **a** deeply disappointed  **e** highly praised
 **b** highly amusing  **f** deeply ashamed
 **c** perfectly reasonable  **g** perfectly happy
 **d** perfectly serious

### Definitions

**4**  **a** feast  **b** landmark  **c** critical  **d** decent
 **e** sensible  **f** hideous  **g** broom

## Grammar

### *used to* and *would*

**5**  **1** used to do / did  **2** found  **3** discovered
 **4** included  **5** used to spend / would spend
 **6** would use / used  **7** confirmed
 **8** used to be / was  **9** used to take / would take / took
 **10** used to be / were  **11** used to walk / would walk
 **12** used to be / were  **13** used to visit / would visit
 **14** estimated

## Unit 9

## Reading

**1**  It is giving them misleading information on product packaging.

**2**  1 E  2 G  3 A  4 D  5 F  6 B

**3**  **a** regulations; rules; code; verdict
 **b** letting ... down; get away with; call on

## Grammar

### Speculation and deduction

**4**  **a** could/might  **b** must  **c** can't  **d** can't/couldn't
 **e** must  **f** could/might

**5**  **1** might have been done by  **5** must have been paid
 **2** looking forward to going  **6** in getting the/their message
 **3** does your uncle do for  **7** would have been able to
 **4** down to planning  **8** made an impression on

## Vocabulary

### Collocations

6 c, f, g and h do not collocate with *broad*; *deep* could be used with c, f and h, and *wide* with g.

7 **a** jingle **b** slogan **c** budget **d** brand

## Unit 10

### Vocabulary

1 1 C   2 B   3 D   4 C
5 A   6 B   7 D   8 A

2 **a** At first   **b** at his best   **c** at once   **d** at least
**e** at war; at (long) last   **f** at risk

### Listening

3 1 C   2 A   3 B   4 B   5 C   6 A   7 C

---

**Recording script** 1️⃣ 06

*You will hear an interview with a science-fiction writer called Jed Stevens. For questions 1–7, choose the best answer (A, B or C).*

*You now have one minute to look at the questions.*

**Interviewer:** Jed Stevens, welcome to the studio. Now, you've been writing successful science fiction for almost three decades, but at what age would you recommend others to start writing it?

**Jed:** That's a good question. I played around with ideas right through my teens, which is fine for your own amusement, but you just don't have the knowledge or scope to take it on seriously until you're out in the world. In your twenties is about right. There are a few writers who have turned to science fiction much later, in retirement, though I see that as risky commercially.

**Interviewer:** So what led you to science fiction in the first place?

**Jed:** Well, it would be convenient to say it was weekly doses of *Star Trek*, which was on television when I was a kid, but in actual fact, I couldn't stand it! My elder brother loved it and he listened to stuff on the radio too, but that didn't work for me – I wanted visual images to stimulate my imagination, and I found them in a colourful comic strip that I consumed every week without fail.

**Interviewer:** And as a writer, is there anything in particular that has been helpful to you?

**Jed:** To create my stories, do you mean? I guess I've got a lot from locations where I've spent some time – I've never lived in one place for more than five years, and unusual environments inspire me. My early work as a programmer was the opposite, no help at all, so I left in the end to follow my dream. Living where I do now, I'm in touch with a lot of scientists, but they're generally too focused on reality to be useful to my brand of fantasy! Interesting people though.

**Interviewer:** You've written 25 novels, but what was the very first publication of yours to come out?

**Jed:** It was hard at the start, you know ... I desperately wanted to get published and I remember I tried with a short story, but everyone said they'd only consider a whole collection, so that was out. Then I decided to enter a competition for first novels but I missed the deadline. (I'm still polishing that novel 30 years later!) No, it was a modest piece in a magazine about life in other galaxies ... from small beginnings, eh?

**Interviewer:** Well, you obviously found the magic ingredient! And what's the attraction now? I'm sure you don't really need the money.

**Jed:** It's always been the same thrill. Science fiction allows you to find fresh angles on how people live and interact. You mentioned earnings, but they were really only necessary while my kids were growing up. Today I get by on next to nothing. I know I could make a lot more if I accepted a role in the filming of my stories, but I'm just not into that side of the business.

**Interviewer:** Jed, if you look back over your 30 years in the business, as you put it, what has changed in science fiction writing?

**Jed:** Strangely enough, given all the technological progress we've seen since the 80s, it's not the storylines themselves that have altered, but the storytelling itself – that's improved hugely, in my view. The other aspect that some people comment on is that the novels have become shorter over the years, but I don't think there's any evidence for that ... not in my case, anyway!

**Interviewer:** OK, and what do you see happening to the human race in the future, say 50 years from now?

**Jed:** Well I don't have a crystal ball but my thoughts are that government funding for space exploration will become more necessary than ever due to a lack of resources on Earth. I don't think people will be able to get beyond our solar system, but I'm certain that unmanned vehicles will be sent that far, with fascinating results. I also believe that we'll have started exploiting distant places for water by then, on an icy moon of Jupiter maybe.

**Interviewer:** Who knows? Jed, it's been really good to talk to you today, thank you.

**Jed:** My pleasure.

---

## Grammar

### Review of future tenses

4 *Suggested answers*
   **a** Within 20 years, a manned spacecraft will have landed on Mars.
   **b** In the 22nd century, it may be possible to launch starships, whose destination would be other galaxies.
   **c** Soon, people will be able to travel to low orbit and the journey time between Europe and New Zealand will be only an hour.

## Writing

5 *Suggested answer*

Between 10 and 12 January, 2020, Elwood College of Technology is hosting a conference on future developments in space. The guest speakers will include, science-fiction writer John T. Price and the leading scientist Professor Paul Rhodes, who will be speaking about his latest research. The discussions will cover topics such as beam-up technology, moon settlements and how to contact aliens.

# Unit 11
## Vocabulary
### Word formation

1  1 personality   2 appearance   3 likely
   4 Scientists   5 relationships   6 choice
   7 social   8 reasonable

2  a nervous/uneasy   afraid   terrified
   b pleased   delighted/thrilled   overjoyed
   c disappointed   unhappy   miserable/depressed
   d interested   fascinated   eager   obsessed
   e surprised   astonished   shocked   speechless
   f attractive   lovely   beautiful   stunning

### American English

3  on the underground
   she got/became really embarrassed

4  1 g   2 f   3 k   4 i   5 j   6 b
   7 e   8 h   9 a   10 c   11 d

## Writing

5  Dear Jody,

Thanks for your letter; it was good to **hear** from you. You'll be pleased **to know** that I've found someone to **share** the flat with. She's called Elena Richmann and she's **an** actress from Canada. I interviewed about 20 people before I **saw** her. She's very **nice** and we really get on well together. Let me **tell** you a bit about her. She's about 1m 50cm in **height** and has short, black, curly hair; in fact she **looks** a bit like your sister! She's incredibly **lively** so she should be fun to have around. We're both interested **in** the same type of films and we seem to have similar tastes **in** music. She hates **cooking** so I won't have to **worry** about having a messy kitchen!

One drawback is that, when she **is** making a movie, she needs **to get** up really early, about 4.30 in the morning, to go to the set to get her make-up and costume sorted out. She says she'll be really **quiet**, so we'll have to see. Anyway, I haven't **noticed any** bad habits yet! You must **meet** her – why don't you come over to the flat next **Saturday** and we can have a meal together? Drop me a line to let me know.
Love,
Tanya

6  *Suggested answer*

Dear Lynne,

I thought I'd write and tell you all my latest news. We've got new neighbours. You remember I told you that we had a large family living next door? Well, the father has got a new job in New York and they moved out last week. They were quite fun, but a bit noisy. They often used to have large family parties and the young children would run around shouting. Their parents and their grandpa and grandma were nice though.

The new neighbours are a family with identical twin girls, aged 15. They're very pretty and, so far, seem quite friendly. I hope I'll be able to tell them apart. Their dad came over yesterday to say hello and we're going to have them over for a barbeque next weekend. I'll write and let you know if my first impression of them was right!

That's all my news for now. Hope you're keeping well.

Love,

# Unit 12
## Reading

1  1 D   2 B   3 A   4 D   5 B   6 D

## Grammar
### The passive

2  a I had to **be trained** by the manager.
   b Usually cuckoo clocks **are made** out of wood.
   c The science exhibition will be **visited** by many people.
   d My camera **was** stolen on the bus.
   e He **had his bike stolen**.
   f It has been **proved** that water freezes at 0 degrees C.
   g French **is spoken** here.
   h Many designs **have been made** for new planes.
   i The house is **being painted** at the moment.
   j The car **is being** cleaned now.
   k Maria **was** born in April.
   l A jet **is flown** by Hamid every day.
   m They were **asked** to a party.
   n Today's meeting **is** cancelled / **has been** cancelled.
   o My house was **built** last year.
   p I **was** hurt in a road accident.

## Vocabulary
### Phrasal verbs with *come* and *take*

3  a inherited   b resembles   c started (a new hobby)
   d regain consciousness   e running   f face/meet
   g like   h produce   i understand/absorb
   j found/discovered (by chance)   k accepting/getting

## Listening

4  1 80   2 mechanic   3 library   4 light   5 water
   6 cousin   7 bicycle   8 plastic   9 TV   10 potatoes

---

**Recording script** 1 07

*You will hear a woman talking about a man called William, who built a windmill in his village in Africa. For questions 1–10, complete the sentences with a word or short phrase.*

*You now have 45 seconds to look at the questions.*

**Woman:** On my radio show today, I'm going to be telling you the amazing story of William. William was born and grew up in a small village in Malawi in Africa. He wasn't

---

naturally academic at school and, in fact, he had to leave school at the age of 14 because his family couldn't afford to pay the $80 tuition fees.

His family were farmers and they wanted William to become one too but William had ambitions to be a mechanic. This looked doubtful because the family had no money and so William had to help out in the fields. He still had some free time though so he would spend it in the local library. There he found two textbooks – *Explaining Physics* and *Using Energy* – and from them, William found out all about how you could get electricity from windmills.

William's village was very poor but it did have a lot of wind. He could see that electricity would solve a number of problems for his family and, best of all, he would be able to have a light in his room so he could read at night.

William could see that having a windmill to make electricity would mean freedom for himself and his family. The electricity would be able to quickly pump water to his family's fields of maize, which would allow them to grow more food.

He decided to build a windmill near his house. His father was too busy so he asked his cousin to help him and they spent some time trying to find the necessary parts. Luckily, they managed to get hold of a bicycle someone had thrown away and which they used to form the basis of the windmill. They mainly used the chain and the dynamo. For the windmill blades they used an old plastic pipe which they cut in two and heated over hot coals to make flat. This all took a long time but the result was worth it.

The windmill was a great success and currently the village has three of them and the villagers can all go to watch TV as well as enjoy all the other benefits electricity has brought. William is now older and is keen to build windmills across the whole of his country. William's family can now harvest other crops besides maize such as potatoes. The people in the village are much healthier and happier than they were before and other children are beginning to study science as they can now see how useful it is to their lives.

## Unit 13
### Reading
**2** 1 E   2 G   3 C   4 A   5 D   6 F

### Grammar
Reporting

**3** **a** Zeinaida said that she had gone to the local paper and had told them their plans. They (had) asked her some questions to check her out, but in the end they (had) promised to run the story.

**b** Chris Searle said that that morning he had gone in through the side entrance. The school secretary was / had been handing out the registers as normal, but there couldn't have been more than 20 or 30 kids in the whole building.

**c** A pupil said that while they were / had been outside the gates, teachers had come across and (had) talked to them. Some were / had been sympathetic, though they weren't / hadn't been able to admit it. Some were / had been aggressive and had thrown gym shoes at them.

**d** Chris Searle said that those children were / had been made to feel that being ordinary meant failure. He argued that it is the ordinary people and their daily work that make a country. (Present tense is used as this is an ongoing truth.)

## Vocabulary
**4** 1 made a good impression   2 make sense of
3 made use of                  4 made their move
5 made their feelings known

**5** **a** make      **e** made        **i** make/made
   **b** had       **f** go on / start  **j** makes/made
   **c** made      **g** take ... make
   **d** do        **h** take

## Unit 14
### Vocabulary
Word formation

**1** 1 selection    5 imaginative
   2 specialise   6 unexpectedly
   3 massive      7 obviously
   4 availability  8 expansion

### Listening
**2** 1 B   2 B   3 A   4 C   5 C

---

**Recording script** **1 08**

*You will hear people talking in five different situations. For questions 1–5, choose the best answer (A, B or C).*

*Question 1*
*You hear a man talking about his working life.*
**Man:** I haven't always been involved in the catering industry. In fact, I trained as a lawyer, although I've never actually worked for a law firm. I spent a few years writing articles for a law magazine, which I quite enjoyed, but I always knew this was what I really wanted to do – the kitchen is my true home! I turned professional last year, after I won a TV competition to find the best amateur in the country. Since then, I've never looked back.

[The recording is repeated.]

*Question 2*
*You hear a conversation about getting a further qualification.*
**Woman:** So I hear you're going back to studying for a while?
**Man:** That's right, it's a full-time course in marketing. My company's going to pay half the fees and I've agreed to work for them for at least a year afterwards in return, though in a different job, obviously.

---

**Woman:** I'm surprised you didn't decide to do something part-time to keep your salary coming in!

**Man:** I thought about it but I'd rather concentrate on the course, to be honest. <u>I've managed to save quite a bit, so I should be OK.</u>

[The recording is repeated.]

*Question 3*

*You hear a woman talking about her career.*

**Woman:** I've been involved in fashion photography for more than ten years now. People are often quite envious of what I do, but it's hard work, with very long days sometimes. It's getting more and more competitive too, so it's hard to make a good living nowadays. Not that it was the money that attracted me in the first place! I suppose <u>I was drawn by the opportunity to visit some exotic locations</u> – that was certainly more important to me than the famous people I'd get the chance to work with.

[The recording is repeated.]

*Question 4*

*You hear two people at work discussing a colleague.*

**Woman:** Mark, can I have a word with you? I'm getting very impatient with Becky.

**Man:** Why's that? I've always found her very easy to get on with.

**Woman:** Well, that's not the problem. She's a lovely person, but whenever I ask her for something, <u>she never seems to know where to look, and takes ages to find what I need</u>. Now she seems to have mislaid a really important file that I gave her last week.

**Man:** OK. Look, I'm responsible for her so I'll have a quiet word – I know she's been a bit overworked recently, but it sounds like she needs to sort herself out a bit.

**Woman:** Thanks Mark, I appreciate it.

**Man:** No problem.

[The recording is repeated.]

*Question 5*

*You hear a man talking about the skills needed for a new position in his department.*

**Man:** This is a new role in the sales and marketing department, to assist in the launch of our latest product range. The post is initially for two years and this help is needed immediately, so we're encouraging internal people to apply. The successful applicant will be given some responsibility for checking costs and updating sales budgets, so although we're not asking for a maths degree, <u>a school-level certificate in that subject is essential</u>. The job will require an element of direct selling by phone, all carried out in English – another language might be an advantage, but we're not demanding that. And we can provide basic training in telephone selling too. Please contact Human Resources if you are interested, as soon as possible.

[The recording is repeated.]

## Writing

5  1 Although     4 In any case     7 To sum up
   2 So             5 On the other hand
   3 in his case     6 Again

## Grammar

*all* and *the whole*

6  a things of all    b whole of    c the whole    d all
   e all of a

# Unit 15
## Vocabulary

1  1 B    2 A    3 B    4 D
   5 B    6 C    7 B    8 A

2  a recycled    b litter      c second-hand
   d drought    e floods    f flash
   g shower     h pollutants    i fossil fuels

## Writing

3  1 As    2 Despite    3 when    4 Besides
   5 So    6 Although    7 because / as a result
   8 as a result    9 though    10 Furthermore

## Grammar

*some, any, no, every*

5  a anything/something      f anywhere
   b anyone/anybody       g anything
   c everywhere           h Everyone/Everybody
   d No one / Nobody      i anything
   e something

# Unit 16
## Reading

1  1 C    2 A    3 B    4 D    5 C
   6 A    7 C    8 B    9 D    10 B

## Listening

2  1 B    2 E    3 D    4 G    5 F

---

**Recording script** 1️⃣09

*You will hear five short extracts in which people are talking about food. For questions 1–5, choose from the list (A–H) what each writer says. Use the letters only once. There are three extra letters which you do not need to use.*

*You now have 30 seconds to look at the questions.*

*Speaker 1*

I tend not to believe people who say they write for eight hours a day. I write for about three hours after breakfast. It's then that my mind is least cluttered. I never eat at my desk. It's messy enough as it is. <u>But food is important to my writing. You can learn about the characters through their attitude to food.</u> Food provokes powerful feelings – a sense of family, for example, when everyone sits down to eat together, or hate, if you take food away from someone, especially a child. In fact, I often write so much about food that my editor has to cut large bits out when she reads it.

*Speaker 2*

I work a long morning – that's when I can be at my most creative. I keep going until I can't do any more. By about two o'clock I realise I'm really hungry and could eat the entire contents of the fridge. One of the great pleasures of working at home is that you can be selfish about eating. I think you have to watch out for food in fiction; it's vital that it doesn't just become some sort of recipe book. I know some writers who just fill the pages with food – their characters seem to eat all the time. I can't do that.

*Speaker 3*

I was born in New York and my grandparents had a restaurant. I really loved their Italian dishes. Ravioli was my favourite and still is. One of the cooks there made great American food too and I used to go back to her home frequently for meals with her family. I based one of my novels on that family – it centres round a detective who has a difficult job but a great happy family. If I'm happy with what I've written in a day, I give myself chocolate. Not too much though as I don't want to pile on the pounds.

*Speaker 4*

I'm not easily distracted by food and I don't see it as something you should have as a reward. For me, it's something that you need to live. As I love writing I spend a lot of time at my desk. I like to start around 9.30 and then work until one. I don't like fancy recipes that take ages to prepare. Something like toast or soup is fine by me. After lunch I have a quick nap and then go shopping or to the library. I then work until seven and watch the news. Later I go out to eat in one of the great restaurants in my area.

*Speaker 5*

When I'm writing, my main character, a detective, takes me over completely. After I get up, I go to the café on the corner and have a coffee, and I used to have a pastry, but not now I'm dieting. Then I sit down and write until about three, not stopping for lunch. Once you start a novel, you don't switch off, so you need pauses to think about what you're going to write next. I used to fill those pauses with chocolate bars but I've managed to stop that now. My character wouldn't cook at all, but I can do a really good beef stew.

## Grammar

### The article

3 a a, the 
  b –, the 
  c the, –, the 
  d An, a, the 
  e a, the, – 
  f –, the, the 
  g a, – 
  h the, the/–

4 1 as   2 so   3 time   4 up 
  5 made   6 order   7 has   8 like

## Unit 17
## Vocabulary
### Word formation

1 1 inclusion 
  2 endless 
  3 competitions 
  4 analysis 
  5 energetic 
  6 unusual 
  7 collection 
  8 Alternatively

2 a swells    c record    e get hooked 
  b kick off    d good causes    f bound

3 a unlikely    c like    e likeable 
  b liking    d likeness

## Writing

4 *Suggested answer*

The haggis, which must be prepared according to the traditional recipe, should be cooled at the time of hurling. The haggis, which will be inspected for illegal firming agents, must not break on landing. A haggis hurler who has the misfortune to see his haggis split will be disqualified. For the junior and middle-weight events, where the haggis should weigh approximately 500 grams, the haggis should be no longer than 22 cm with a maximum diameter of 18 cm.

## Grammar

5 1 it/this   2 to   3 be   4 a 
  5 whose   6 no   7 where/when 
  8 which

## Unit 18
## Reading

1 1 D   2 F   3 A   4 C   5 G   6 B

## Vocabulary

2

| F | T | H | R | I | L | L | E | R | A | N | E |
|---|---|---|---|---|---|---|---|---|---|---|---|
| I | L | L | U | S | T | R | A | T | I | O | N |
| C | T | P | A | O | T | C | L | E | O | V | N |
| T | R | U | C | X | C | H | A | P | T | E | R |
| I | H | B | T | L | R | A | N | H | I | L | P |
| O | N | L | I | C | K | R | Y | T | U | I | L |
| N | B | I | O | G | R | A | P | H | Y | S | O |
| W | E | S | N | C | S | C | E | N | E | T | T |
| Y | O | H | R | A | O | T | T | F | T | N | L |
| K | E | E | H | L | M | E | V | E | N | T | A |
| X | O | R | A | M | I | R | E | V | I | E | W |
| W | E | S | T | O | R | Y | O | P | L | A | Y |

## Grammar

*enough, too, very, so, such*

**3**  **a**  I have never read **such a** long book as this one.

 **b**  The story was **so** complicated that I gave up.

 **c**  Hardback books are (**much**) **too** expensive.

 **d**  **Not** enough books **were** ordered.

 **e**  I was **so/very** sad to hear of the novelist's death.

 **f**  It was **such an** exciting plot.

 **g**  The print in this paperback isn't **big enough**.

 **h**  Characters **such** as these are quite unusual.

**4**  **1**  very  **2**  too  **3**  too  **4**  very  **5**  so
 **6**  such  **7**  enough  **8**  such  **9**  very  **10**  too
 **11**  so  **12**  very  **13**  enough  **14**  such  **15**  too

## Listening

**5**  **1** C  **2** B  **3** C  **4** A  **5** A  **6** B  **7** C

---

### Recording script  ①⑩

*You will hear a radio interview with a woman who has done a survey on attitudes to ebooks. For questions 1–7, choose the best answer (A, B or C).*

*You now have one minute to look at the questions.*

**Interviewer:** Here with me today is Anna Sinclair. Now Anna, you've recently carried out an investigation into people's reading habits and current attitudes to the downloading of ebooks. Whose idea was this?

**Anna:** It was something I wanted to do at university, but my tutor advised me not to due to the work involved. When I graduated, I approached a small market research company, who were interested but said they couldn't finance it immediately. So I applied for a bank loan and sold the results back to the company six months later.

**Interviewer:** Did anything surprise you in your survey findings?

**Anna:** Yes. I had expected that people of my age would be the strongest group in favour of ebooks, but in fact, they had rather mixed feelings, mainly due to cost issues on the hardware needed. Adults in their 40s and 50s with spare income seem to have welcomed the development and it is only the non-computer-literate who refuse to consider ebooks, not surprisingly.

**Interviewer:** And what do people out there see as the biggest advantage of ebooks?

**Anna:** There are so many benefits to ebooks, including easy access to information online no matter where you live and the way you can alter the appearance of the text to suit you. The thing that comes up in the survey above all is volume, the fact that you can carry a whole library around on a piece of hardware that will slip into your pocket.

**Interviewer:** Interesting. Turning to the commercial aspect in all this, how do book publishers view ebooks nowadays?

**Anna:** I've interviewed several people in the industry, who were understandably nervous to begin with, seeing ebooks as a threat to their traditional business. But in fact, just as music downloads have added to album sales, ebooks have provided publishers with a totally new market. I think it's unlikely that paperbacks will disappear but with rising paper costs and transport on top, heavier hardback books look set to die out – even libraries are switching to digital downloads of these, it seems.

**Interviewer:** I see. And what about us, the consumers? Are there no disadvantages?

**Anna:** I wouldn't say that. I don't agree with the argument that reading ebooks is bad for you – some people claim that it leads to weight gain, but doesn't reading a book also involve sitting still? For those people who dislike reading on screen, there will be the added expense of printing and even then, you end up with a pile of paper rather than a solid physical book. But that's about it! Think of the multi-media features that some ebooks include for the same money – audio and photographs, for example.

**Interviewer:** Anna, how do you see ebooks changing the lives of authors – the people who produce them in the first place?

**Anna:** I think it's good news for them, and for their agents, who still have a role to play in relation to the media. And ebooks provide undiscovered writers with the chance to deliver their work to the public, rather than waiting for a willing publisher. As with many electronic products, there are of course opportunities for illegal activity, where the author earns nothing, but it won't impact on their earnings any more than the invention of the photocopier has done already.

**Interviewer:** Yes indeed. Finally, Anna, where will this research take you next in terms of your career?

**Anna:** Well, I've got no plans to do anything else on ebooks at the moment, but the whole area of market research is fascinating, and I want to take it further, maybe even having my own company one day. It's a very competitive field but I've learnt a lot from this experience and I believe I can offer companies a solid service, working in partnership with them.

**Interviewer:** OK, well I wish you every success with it all. Many thanks, Anna Sinclair.

## Unit 19

### Reading

1  1 B    2 C    3 D    4 B    5 A    6 D

### Vocabulary

2  **a** attendance    **f** confident
   **b** choice    **g** weekly
   **c** fitness    **h** social
   **d** disruptive    **i** effective
   **e** manageable    **j** suitable

3
| B | A | N | D | A | G | E | B | H | L |
|---|---|---|---|---|---|---|---|---|---|
| G | N | D | H | W | A | L | L | C | Q |
| U | K | I | G | I | T | B | K | A | S |
| F | L | U | U | A | B | O | R | M | T |
| Y | E | R | O | Y | N | W | T | O | K |
| M | H | R | C | U | E | N | D | T | N |
| S | H | A | O | L | X | I | F | S | E |
| T | E | H | E | A | D | A | C | H | E |
| Q | R | Y | M | L | D | P | V | N | O |
| I | N | J | E | C | T | I | O | N | P |

### Grammar

4  1 high time you stopped
   2 do/would you advise me to
   3 I were you, I would
   4 suggested going / suggested that we/they (should) go
   5 to have your teeth checked
   6 (high) time you had/got your
   7 had better not sit

### Writing

5  *Suggested answer*

I think that there has never been a better time to be fit and healthy. For a start, supermarkets make a point of including calorie counts on all their food so that you know exactly how much salt, sugar and fat you are eating. If you believe that being a vegetarian is healthier than eating meat then you will have no problem finding ready meals or restaurants which suit your style of eating.

More and more people are joining gyms or going running or doing pilates classes. There really is no excuse for not being able to keep fit as every town has its own gym or sports centre or swimming pool, and these places are often reasonably priced.

If you don't fancy keeping fit with other people, then get a bike and go out riding. I do this quite a bit – I always cycle to college. I never get the bus because it is very expensive and I would have to wait a long time for one to come along. In the past, it may have been difficult to keep fit and healthy, but certainly not nowadays.

## Unit 20

### Listening

1  1 medicine    6 footprints
   2 professor    7 microscope
   3 murderers    8 fog
   4 magazine    9 historical
   5 chemistry    10 furniture

---

**Recording script** 1 11

*You will hear a student called Dan talking about the famous detective Sherlock Holmes, who was created by the writer Sir Arthur Conan Doyle. For questions 1–10, complete the sentences with a word or short phrase.*

*You now have 45 seconds to look at the questions.*

**Dan:** OK, for my presentation on crime, I want to talk about Sir Arthur Conan Doyle and his character the detective Sherlock Holmes, who I really like reading about. Conan Doyle was born in 1859 in Edinburgh, Scotland, and was greatly influenced by his mother's love of storytelling. However, rather than studying literature, from 1876 to 1881 he did <u>medicine</u> at the University of Edinburgh.

Although Conan Doyle began writing short stories during his time at university, it wasn't until he had graduated and set up a medical practice in London that he began to write seriously. This was because he wasn't a particularly successful doctor and had very few patients. His main inspiration for the character of Sherlock Holmes was a <u>professor</u> who had taught him at Edinburgh.

Another inspiration for his writing was a visit Conan Doyle had made at the age of 15 to a wax museum in London. There were wax models of well-known actors and singers there, but it was the models of famous <u>murderers</u> that had the greatest impact on him.

The character Sherlock Holmes first appeared in 1887, not in a novel but as a short story called *A Study in Scarlet* in a <u>magazine</u>. Holmes was a private detective who ran an agency from his apartment at 221B Baker Street in London and shared most of his work with his friend Dr Watson. From the books Conan Doyle wrote, I've learnt that Holmes had an expert knowledge of <u>chemistry</u>, but wasn't quite so good at biology.

Sherlock Holmes was one of the first detectives in fiction to make use of forensic medicine. He was particularly good at identifying <u>footprints</u> at a crime scene. These techniques were fairly new when Conan Doyle was writing, but they later formed a key part of actual detective work.

I always knew Holmes used a magnifying glass for finding small pieces of evidence such as hair or ash, but what amazed me was that he also used a <u>microscope</u>. What he didn't use was photography, which was commonly used at the time by the police to record accident scenes and the faces of criminals – it's strange that Conan Doyle doesn't mention it at all in the stories.

Conan Doyle used London as a setting for many of his Sherlock Holmes stories, and the way he describes the city at that time is fantastic. Many modern-day readers of his stories find it odd that there's no <u>fog</u> nowadays! This was a real problem for Londoners until the 1950s when the burning of coal was forbidden.

Conan Doyle wrote his first set of stories about Holmes over a ten-year period. After this, he became more interested in writing <u>historical</u> novels rather than detective fiction and so he killed off Sherlock Holmes in a book published in 1893. But, in 1901, Conan Doyle gave in to public pressure and wrote some more books about Holmes.

If you're a fan of Sherlock Holmes, then you can visit an interesting museum in London dedicated to him. It is situated at 239 Baker Street. It tries hard to recreate the apartment that Holmes and Watson lived in but, although some details like the violin case and pipe are accurate, the museum has been criticised for displaying the wrong type of <u>furniture</u>. You can also find a small exhibition hall and a gift shop there.

So, any questions? …

## Vocabulary
### Word formation

2
1 popularity
2 differences
3 burglary
4 relatively
5 conventional
6 increasing
7 equality
8 regardless

## Grammar

3
1 what
2 since
3 As
4 would
5 so
6 like
7 on
8 little

### Gerunds or infinitives 2

4
a He suggested **buying** a detective novel.
b I look forward to **hearing** the results of the case.
c Correct
d The burglar alarm needs **looking** at.
e Let me **give** you a description of the mugger.
f Correct
g I can't afford **to take** a taxi all the time just to avoid the underground.
h The tourist was accustomed to **driving** his car faster in his country.
i You are not allowed **to drop** litter on the street.
j I'd like **to report** a burglary.
k Correct

## Writing

5
1 assess
2 document
3 without
4 written
5 physical
6 which
7 consists
8 measurable
9 although
10 impressively
11 accepted
12 psychology

## Unit 21
### Reading

1 b

2 1 D  2 A  3 B  4 F  5 C  6 G

3

| Verb | Noun |
|------|------|
| adapt | adaptability |
| harmonise | harmony |
| locate | location |
| produce | productivity |
| promote | promotion |
| provide | provision, provider |
| respond | response |

## Grammar
### Mixed conditionals

4
1 e (mixed conditional)
2 c (second conditional)
3 a (mixed conditional)
4 f (third conditional)
5 d (mixed conditional)
6 b (mixed conditional)

## Vocabulary
### Word formation

5
1 existence
2 location
3 successful
4 requirements
5 funding
6 regeneration
7 unlikely
8 reconsidered

## Unit 22
### Vocabulary

1
1 D   5 B
2 B   6 D
3 C   7 A
4 C   8 C

2
a performance – not a musical instrument
b conductor – not playing an instrument
c rehearsal – not the final performance
d key – not something that is composed
e compose – not part of a live performance
f orchestra – much larger group than the others
g stage – something within a physical space
h cello – one instrument as opposed to an orchestra section

## Writing

3 1 C   2 E   3 A   4 B   5 F   6 D

## Listening

4 1 C   2 B   3 A   4 B   5 A   6 C

## Recording script ① 12

*You will hear people talking in six different situations. For questions 1–6, choose the best answer (A, B or C).*

*Question 1*

*You hear a professional musician talking about his work.*

**Man:** I've been a member of this <u>orchestra</u> for the last six years – I play the double bass. In my student days I was a bass guitarist in a band that did covers of all the top songs, but I don't get the chance to do that any more. Our schedule's pretty tough because we do a lot of concerts abroad. When I'm not touring, I try to get to a few jazz gigs, just to see how my instrument is being played.

[The recording is repeated.]

*Question 2*

*You hear a man and a woman talking about a band.*

**Woman:** That was a great concert we went to on Saturday. I've just downloaded their new album, by the way.

**Man:** Have you? And is it as good as the last one?

**Woman:** Not sure yet – it's very different. There's nothing familiar from their concert either! <u>The lyrics contain some really powerful images</u> though, worth listening to properly.

**Man:** Sounds like it will take a bit of time to get into it. Can I borrow it sometime?

**Woman:** Yeah, OK.

[The recording is repeated.]

*Question 3*

*You hear a boy and a girl talking about their guitar lessons.*

**Boy:** How are you getting on with your guitar classes this term?

**Girl:** It's fun. We've got a new book and the pieces are a lot longer than before, so I'm having to do more practice. How about you?

**Boy:** Not too good. There are too many in our class now – it used to be just four, but now, with eight of us, <u>I don't feel I'm making as much progress</u> somehow, even though I do loads of practice.

**Girl:** Well you should ask to move to our class. You're free on Wednesday evenings, aren't you?

**Boy:** I am, that's a good idea, thanks.

[The recording is repeated.]

*Question 4*

*You hear part of a radio interview with a female singer.*

**Man:** So you're able to make a good living from your music, which is fantastic. What part of your work earns you the most, would you say?

**Woman:** Well it used to be the case that my recordings brought in a lot, especially the ones I did without my backing band, but with so much downloading and file sharing, that side has dropped a bit.

**Man:** And how about your live appearances with the band – you play some very big venues, don't you?

**Woman:** Yes, but when we tour there's never much profit from the ticket sales once all our expenses have been paid. Where I've been really lucky recently is being approached to record a couple of my own things for <u>TV commercials, and they bring in an absolute fortune!</u> Just singing solo, which I love best.

[The recording is repeated.]

*Question 5*

*You hear a composer talking about his latest work.*

**Man:** It's been a challenge to get the piece finished but I'm happy with how it has turned out. I hope it will influence the next generation of composers – I see in my own students that they need to think outside the box if they are to deliver truly modern music. The piece is going to be performed for the first time next month in New York, which is appropriate, as it was <u>the daily noise of the traffic and the crowds there that proved to be such a major contribution to the mood of the piece</u>. The whole use of percussion and brass comes from that experience, so different from the peaceful farm where I grew up.

[The recording is repeated.]

*Question 6*

*You hear a man and a woman talking about an open-mic night.*

**Woman:** Hi, Chris. I missed the open-mic night this week – how was it?

**Man:** Great. The house band was good, although their bass guitarist wasn't up to his usual high standard. I think he may have been ill.

**Woman:** Oh dear. And did that Scottish girl with the electric violin play again? Hers was the best performance by far last time.

**Man:** Sadly not – she doesn't live in the village, you know. <u>The real highlight was this teenage kid who brought his keyboard along</u>. He was a bit nervous so he just played with the band to begin with, but then they let him do two of his own songs. He's got a future in music, I'd say.

**Woman:** There're so many talented musicians around here.

**Man:** Yeah. We're very lucky.

[The recording is repeated.]

## Unit 23

### Vocabulary

1

| Y | L | I | G | H | T | N | I | N | G |
|---|---|---|---|---|---|---|---|---|---|
| F | Z | T | V | U | T | N | K | R | O |
| L | H | H | O | S | S | N | O | W | S |
| O | X | U | S | T | O | R | M | A | F |
| O | Z | N | J | Q | K | O | U | I | L |
| D | I | D | S | H | O | W | E | R | A |
| K | E | E | Q | I | R | E | D | N | S |
| F | O | R | E | C | A | S | T | A | H |
| O | I | R | A | I | N | D | R | O | P |
| H | U | R | R | I | C | A | N | E | E |

2 a hurricanes    d storm    g thunder
   b snow    e raindrops    h forecast
   c flash ... lightning    f showers    i flood(s)

### Reading

3 a F    b T    c T    d T

5   1 C    3 A    5 D    7 F    9 D
   2 E    4 B    6 C    8 A    10 B

6 a inside      f unlucky
   b recalling      g complete
   c enormous      h occasionally
   d upper      i positive
   e sensible/careful      j freezing

### Grammar

*I wish / If only*

7 a I hope I **will** see you soon. / I hope **to** see you soon.
   b I wish I **could** go to visit you.
   c Correct
   d Correct
   e If only you **managed** to give up smoking, just think of the money you'd save.
   f I hope the weather **stays / will stay** nice for you.
   g Correct
   h I wish I **hadn't** seen that film about earthquakes – I can't sleep at night now.
   i Correct
   j Dave wishes he **knew** more about earthquakes.

## Unit 24

### Vocabulary

Word formation

1   1 comedians      5 products
   2 substantial      6 viewers
   3 entertainment      7 difference
   4 similar      8 endings

2 a pay   b court   c pay   d not

### Listening

3   1 B    2 C    3 A    4 C    5 B    6 A    7 C

---

**Recording script** 1️⃣ 13

*You will hear an interview with a comedian called Kate Gordon. For questions 1–7, choose the best answer (A, B or C).*

*You now have one minute to look at the questions.*

**Interviewer:** Here with me now is Kate Gordon, who has just won a comedy award at a major festival. Kate, what was the award for exactly?

**Kate:** My one-woman stand-up show! I'm delighted as I've never been sure I could do it, but the festival audiences thought otherwise. Up till now, I've usually been part of something bigger – the radio show was with six talented comedians, and my earlier work as a TV script-writer also involved a large team.

**Interviewer:** And is there anything particularly challenging about being a female comedian?

**Kate:** Well, there are far more guys out there doing shows, which could put some women off, I suppose, but it's never stopped me! New venues are opening up, too, so it's becoming a bit easier to get regular bookings around the country. Having said that, it wouldn't be a very attractive lifestyle touring on my own if and when I have kids!

**Interviewer:** You write most of your own material. Does that side come easily to you?

**Kate:** Definitely not. It involves a lot of time and effort. It's not possible to develop a series of new jokes overnight, and even when I've written something that's half OK, I'll still need to try it out in front of an audience a couple of times before it's really right. And actually, sometimes I'm quite surprised by the weird sense of humour that people have. They're more extreme than I am!

**Interviewer:** And where do your best ideas come from?

**Kate:** For my jokes? They come from me, of course! I guess my recipe for success is to be very nosy – I observe everyone I come into contact with, apart from my friends, that is, who would never allow me to get material from their lives! I never find stuff on the internet either – it has to come from daily things that are happening around me, and I don't miss much!

**Interviewer:** Several comedians have found success in the cinema. Would that ever interest you?

**Kate:** Maybe. I'd enjoy the teamwork for sure, being part of something big. It would have to be the right project though – too many comedians seem to end up with second-rate scripts, which doesn't help your career in the long run. I think I'd want to have some control over the writing, even if I couldn't do it myself. And I'd be looking for a young director willing to try things differently.

**Interviewer:** Do you ever get nervous in front of an audience?

**Kate:** I'd be lying if I said no! I think it's quite natural to experience some anxiety, but for me, the strange thing is that I feel much more secure in front of a really big audience, even if it's a massive one outdoors. <u>While if there're only 40 or so in a tiny club, it's easy to lose your confidence if you catch someone's eye at the wrong moment.</u> I suppose the easiest place for me is the theatre down the road, where most people know me.

**Interviewer:** Finally Kate, how would you advise people to get going in comedy?

**Kate:** Well, don't make the mistake of just looking at others doing their shows – <u>you've got to find out pretty early on whether you can handle doing a live act, so the way forward is to try an open-mic night,</u> where you get the chance to do a short performance for real people. You won't do brilliantly to begin with but if you keep practising, you'll either improve or realise that it's not for you.

**Interviewer:** OK, well thanks very much Kate.

**Kate:** No worries, it was fun.

## Grammar

4  1  put up with
   2  rather see live comedy than
   3  turn/switch off our computers as/because
   4  insisted on knowing the contents
   5  had got the sack
   6  would rather not stay/wait

# Acknowledgements

Development of this publication has made use of the Cambridge English Corpus (CEC). The CEC is a computer database of contemporary spoken and written English, which currently stands at over one billion words. It includes British English, American English and other varieties of English. It also includes the Cambridge Learner Corpus, developed in collaboration with Cambridge English Language Assessment. Cambridge University Press has built up the CEC to provide evidence about language use that helps to produce better language teaching materials.

This product is informed by the English Vocabulary Profile, built as part of English Profile, a collaborative programme designed to enhance the learning, teaching and assessment of English worldwide. Its main funding partners are Cambridge University Press and Cambridge English Language Assessment and its aim is to create a 'profile' for English linked to the Common European Framework of Reference for Languages (CEF). English Profile outcomes, such as the English Vocabulary Profile, will provide detailed information about the language that learners can be expected to demonstrate at each CEF level, offering a clear benchmark for learners' proficiency. For more information, please visit www.englishprofile.org

**The authors and publishers acknowledge the following sources of copyright material and are grateful for the permissions granted. While every effort has been made, it has not always been possible to identify the sources of all the material used, or to trace all copyright holders. If any omissions are brought to our notice, we will be happy to include the appropriate acknowledgements on reprinting.**

The Guardian for the text on p. 5 adapted from 'Levi's Jeans' *The Guardian* 13.3.97, for the text on p. 6 adapted from 'Board Games' by Stuart Miller, *The Guardian* 26.7.97, for the text on p. 10 adapted from 'The frozen zoo' by Paul Harris, *The Guardian* 29.8.10, for the text on p. 20 adapted from 'Food Labels' by Roger Cowe, *The Guardian* 10.11.97, for the text on p. 28 adapted from 'Return of a class hero' by Andy Beckett, *The Guardian* 19.11.97, for the text on p. 38 adapted from 'Daphne du Maurier' by Patrick McGrath, *The Guardian* 5.5.07, for the text on p. 40 adapted from 'On the hoof to heal' by Emily Sheffield, *The Guardian* 23.12.97, for the text on p. 46 adapted from 'Steven Poole's guide to sonic tools that shaped pop', by Steven Poole, *The Guardian* 15.1.99. Copyright Guardian News & Media Ltd; News Syndication for the text on p. 16 adapted from 'Discover a World beneath the Ice' by Nicholas Roe, *The Times* 2.1.10, for the text on p. 19 adapted from 'Lazy Generation' by Steve Conner and Edward Welch, *The Times* 1.6.97. Copyright © News Syndication; The Independent for the text on p. 22 adapted from 'Space tourism: we have lift off' by Stephen Foley, *The Independent* 25.3.10. Copyright © The Independent; Condé Nast Publications for the listening exercise on p. 27 adapted from 'Teen's DIY energy hacking gives African village new hope' by Kim Zetter, 2.10.09. Copyright © 2009 Condé Nast Publications. All rights reserved. Originally published in Wired.com. Reprinted by permission; IPC Syndication for the text on p. 30 adapted from 'Tile Art', *Woman & Home* February 1997. Copyright © Woman & Home/IPC Syndication; Telegraph Media Group Limited for the text on

p. 31 adapted from 'Nick D'Aloisio, Britain's 17 year old app entrepreneur' by Mark Sutherland, The Telegraph 26.3.13. Copyright © Telegraph Media Group Limited 2013; John Brown for the listening exercise on p. 35 adapted from 'Hungry Minds' by Ian Rankin, *Waitrose Food Illustrated*, February 2004. Copyright © John Brown; Text on p. 35 adapted from 'Ken Hom' *The Telegraph*, 12.4.97; Professor Ken Worpole for the text on p. 44 adapted from 'Time and the City', (originally published in *Town & Country* April 1998). Reproduced with permission of Professor Ken Worpole; Candis Magazine for the text on p. 49 from 'Lightning Strikes' by Deborah Dooley, *Candis Magazine* February 1998. Copyright © Candis Magazine.

**Photo acknowledgements:**
p. 5 ©Dith Pran/NYT/Redux/Eyevine; p. 6 (L): Indexstock/Superstock; p. 6 (R): Kuttig – People – 2/Alamy; p. 8 Shutterstock/Kathleen Struckle; p. 9 iStockphoto.com/fototrav; p. 10 Robert Harding World Imagery/Alamy; p. 16 Poelzer Wolfgang/Alamy; p. 18 michaeljung/Shutterstock; p. 19 (TR): George Marks/Hulton Archive/ Getty Images; p. 19 (BR):Belinda Images/Superstock; p. 19 (TL): Topfoto; p. 19 (BL): Noel Hendrickson/Getty Images; p. 24 (R, L): JupiterimagesThinkstock; p. 24 (CR): leungchopan/ Shutterstock; p. 24 (CL): StockbyteThinkstock; p. 25 (A): Ryan McVay/Thinkstock; p. 25 (B): Radius/Superstock; p. 26 Cody Images/USAF; p. 27 ullstein bild/Sven Simon/Topfoto; p. 31: Suzanne Plunkett/Reuters/Corbis; p. 32 Sygma/B.Bission/Corbis; p. 34 (A): Amos Morgan Thinkstock; p. 34 (B): Photodisc Thinkstock; p. 34 (C): Roy Botterell/Getty Images; p. 34 (D): Creatas Images Thinkstock; p. 35 Nils Jorgensen/Rex Features; p. 36 (TL, TR): Trevor Clifford; p. 36 (B): The Scotsman Publications Ltd; p. 37 Photo, Regia Anglorum - www.regia.org; p. 38 Mary Evans Picture Library; p. 40 wildscape/Alamy; p. 44 (T): Kathy deWitt/Alamy; p. 44 (B): Richard Levine/Alamy; p. 47 Gerard Hancock/Art Directors & TRIP; p. 48 Comstock Thinkstock; p. 50 Salisbury Newspaper.

**Illustrations:**
Kathy Baxendale p. 20; Dominic Bugatto p. 42; Nick Duffy pp. 12, 30; Katie Mac p. 22; Julian Mosedale pp. 46, 50; Jorge Santillan p. 14; Kipper Williams p. 5 (B)

Recordings produced by Ian Harker, Ian Harker Audio, with Paul Deeley at The Soundhouse Ltd.

Picture research by Kevin Brown.

The authors would like to thank Bartosz Michałowski for his thorough and constructive editing on this 4th edition, and Joanne Hunter, Lorraine Poulter and Lynn Townsend for their in-house support and encouragement.

**The publisher has used its best endeavours to ensure that the URLs for external websites referred to in this book are correct and active at the time of going to press. However, the publisher has no responsibility for the websites and can make no guarantee that a site will remain live or that the content is or will remain appropriate.**